I0814138

# CARLOS FERRATER

Cover image: 3 Housing Blocks in Cerda's Enchanche. Photo by Joan Guillamat

# Ferrater & Partners

**OAB**
OFFICE OF
ARCHITECTURE
IN BARCELONA

# CARLOS FERRATER

in his studio, together with his only employee. There I could draw the pictures of some apartments in El Garraf he was designing, as well as a detached house that I would see built years later in Llerona.

In the last year of my university course, I had Roberto Terradas as professor. That year, we designed a hotel of remarkable size and complexity. As my tutor I chose Norman Cinnamond, a young admirer of Federico Correa, who, at that time, was doing good work in interior design projects. With him, I was able to work as an architect on the annual Hogar Hotel pavilion, reserved each year for the best interior designers in Barcelona.

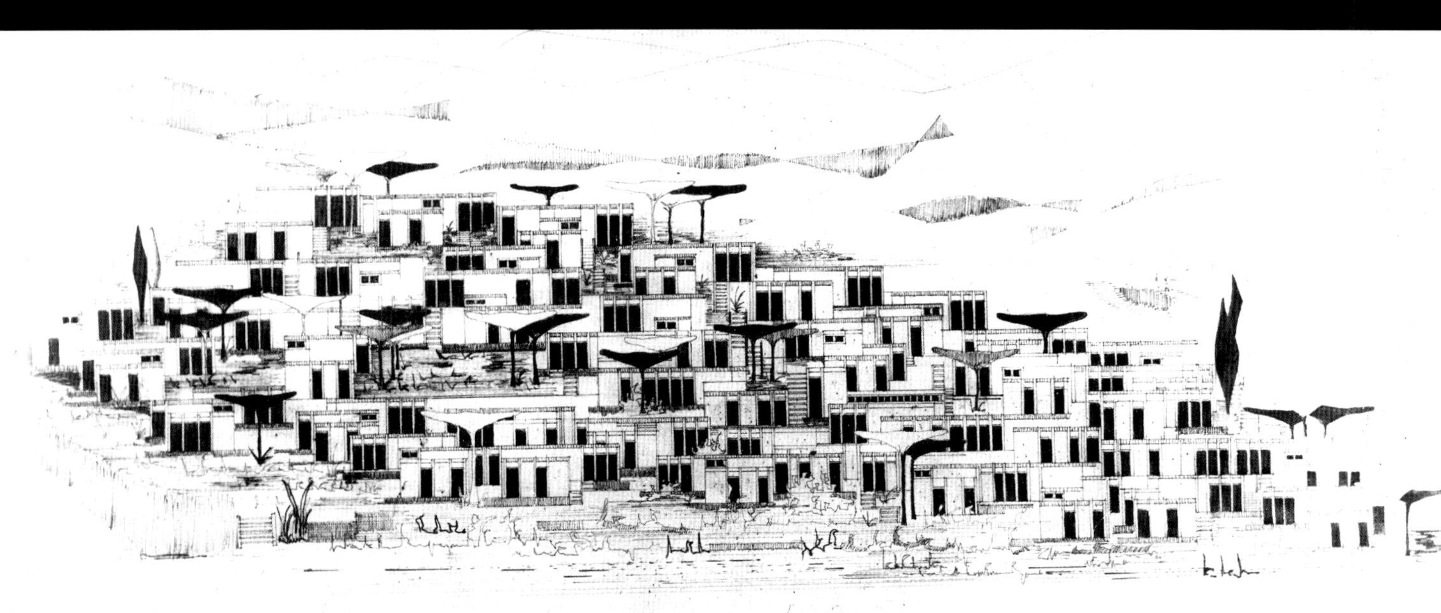

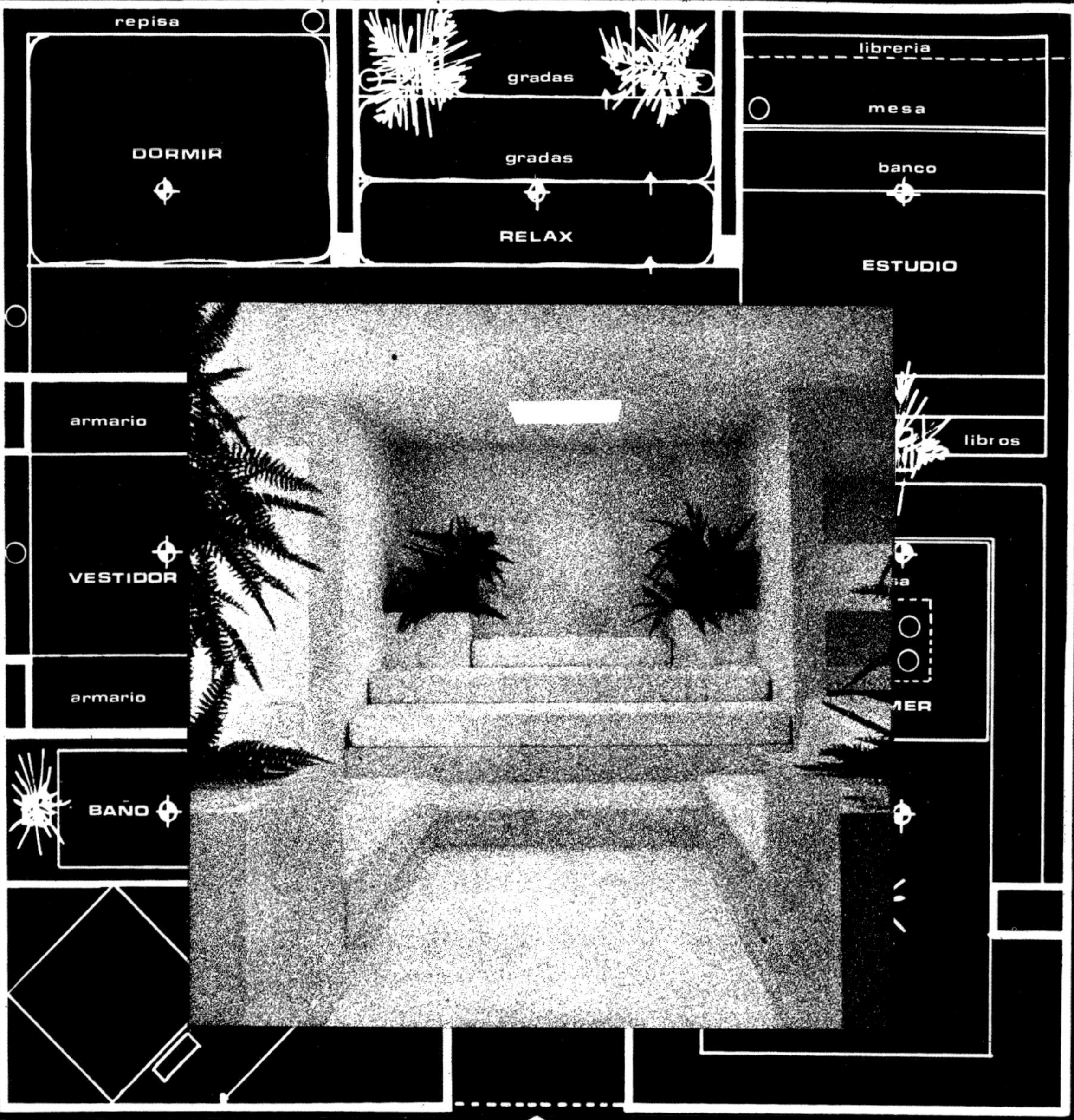


Stand Hogarhotel. Early 70's. Norman Cinnamond - Carlos Ferrater

From that time, I can remember only two good lectures, much anticipated but not all that well attended by students. At the first of these, Richard Neutra, who was in the city and who spoke about architecture and nature, explained the second Kaufmann residence in Palm Springs. The first Kaufmann residence, Falling Water, had been designed by Frank Lloyd Wright a few years earlier. In the second lecture, Javier Sáez de Oiza showed his design for houses in Alcúdia and talked mainly about astronomy, which was the subject that interested him at that time.

As for the others, from those years at the school I remember some interesting but almost incomprehensible classes in descriptive geometry by Professor Canosa; some magnificent lessons on structures by Professor Bordoy, classes in which his particular right-wing ideology was evident; some colloquiums on mathematics by the wise Professor Pi Calleja, and very little else.

During those years, José Antonio Coderch was briefly present as lecturer in designs from the new 1964 plan and, although his classes were not part of my course, I decided to go to tutorials with very few students and to do the course exercise. This consisted of designing a detached house in El Maresme in a housing development where he had to build his commissions in those difficult years for good architecture. After two weeks of hard work, I presented the drawings of a house which for me was very “Coderchian”. I was quite proud of it, but after Coderch had corrected it, nothing was left standing.

Looking at my name in the box he told me: “Ferrater, this is all wrong. Your project is unstructured and disorganised. Sort it out.” That was all he said. I asked him what I could do to understand how I should redo it. He replied: “Look, I’ve built some houses. Visit them, look at them carefully and learn.” There, my opportunity ended. I visited his houses and that was my real learning experience during those years. In this way, Coderch became my “invisible friend”, as I would never have the chance to work in his small studio. I learned many things from those visits. I began with the 1956 Catasús House in Sitges, then the 1961 Uriach House in Ametlla del Vallès, followed by the 1962 Rozés House in Roses and finally the 1965 Gili House in Sitges.

Sometime later, I visited the Ugalde House on several occasions. When I finished my formal studies, I had the opportunity to spend a weekend with Inés de Arquer at the Senillosa house in Cadaqués. It was a small house in the urban area next to Alguer beach based on Mediterranean vernacular architecture. However, with its abstraction and the formal definition of its floor plan and sections, it incorporated the contemporary appearance that I wanted for those new times and it became the key element for my future training.

Drawing a sigle family house for the professor J.A. Coderch during the first year of the University

## Coderch Home Studio in Plaza Calvó

In 2004, Lucía Ferrater was commissioned to renovate what had been José Antonio Coderch de Sentmenat's last home and studio, abandoned and greatly deteriorated in Barcelona's Plaza de Calvó.

After a careful and exhaustive study of the building and its garden, I believe Lucía carried out an impeccable renovation, which was not easy as she had to adapt the house, studio and garden to the needs of the new times in terms of facilities and services. She did all this without altering all the essential aspects of the work Coderch had done.

Senillosa House. J.A. Coderch. COAC Historical archive. Photo: Català-Roca

Coderch de Sentmenat House-Studio in Plaza Calvó of Barcelona. 2004. Lucía Ferrater

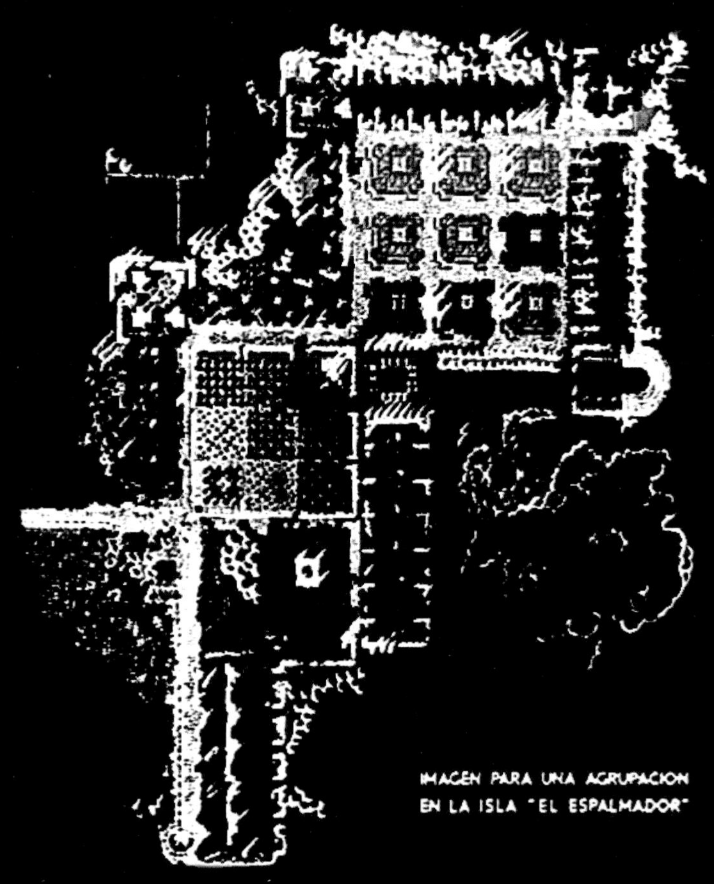


Proposal for “El Espalmador” island. Norma Cinnamond - Carlos Ferrater

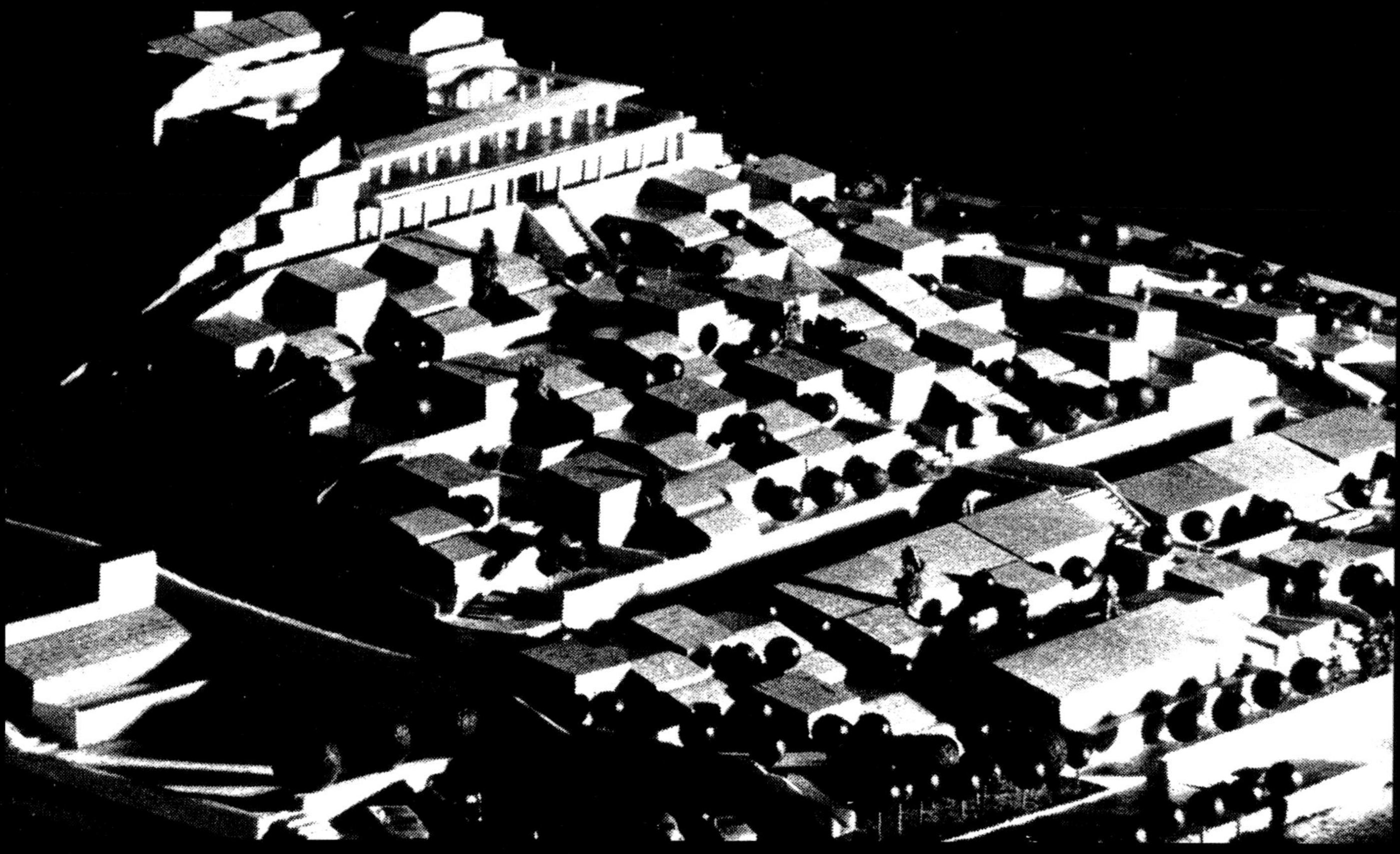

Proposal for a village in a Javea’s hill. Early 70’s

Other influences I had in that period of learning included visits to the Taller de Arquitectura with Anna Bofill, with whom I shared the last years of my course, as well as with Peter Hodgkinson, when I met him was playing the drums at Pierre Lotier's guest house in Cadaqués.

I also had a professional relationship with Javier Bagué Bofill, partner and cousin of Ricardo Bofill, who had just left the Taller de Arquitectura. In his last years there, he had worked on the Gaudí district project in Reus.

At that time, my interest was focused on the drawings and models of the City in Space that Ricardo and his colleagues were planning for Madrid. This interest was reinforced on the study trip I made with a classmate along the Spanish coast all the way from Huelva to the Pyrenees to see vernacular architecture in situ, along with some good projects carried out in more recent years. In Calpe, I visited and enjoyed the apartment complexes that the Taller de Arquitectura had just completed, and we particularly appreciated the La Manzanera complex and the Muralla Roja.

This experience led me to study the urban, utopian and futuristic architectures that were being developed at that time in various countries around the world. I created a document that grouped the different families that at the time were of greatest interest to me by architects such as Yona Friedman; Paolo Soleri and his integrated theatre; Jean-Paul Jungmann and his pneumatic cells that could be applied quickly in the Instant City; the metabolic architecture of Kisho Kurokawa; Cousteau and his cities under the sea; Buckminster Fuller covering Manhattan with a geodesic dome; the Herron City; Dynapolis; Radio City by Justus Dahinden; the Stepped City; Paul Maymont's floating cities; and the Plug-In City of Archigram and Peter Cook. This architect was invited by our year to ETSAB a few years later, together with Cedric Price, who designed the London Zoo aviary.

Experimenting with geodesic shapes in Vallvidrera. José María Berenguer & Carlos Gutiérrez

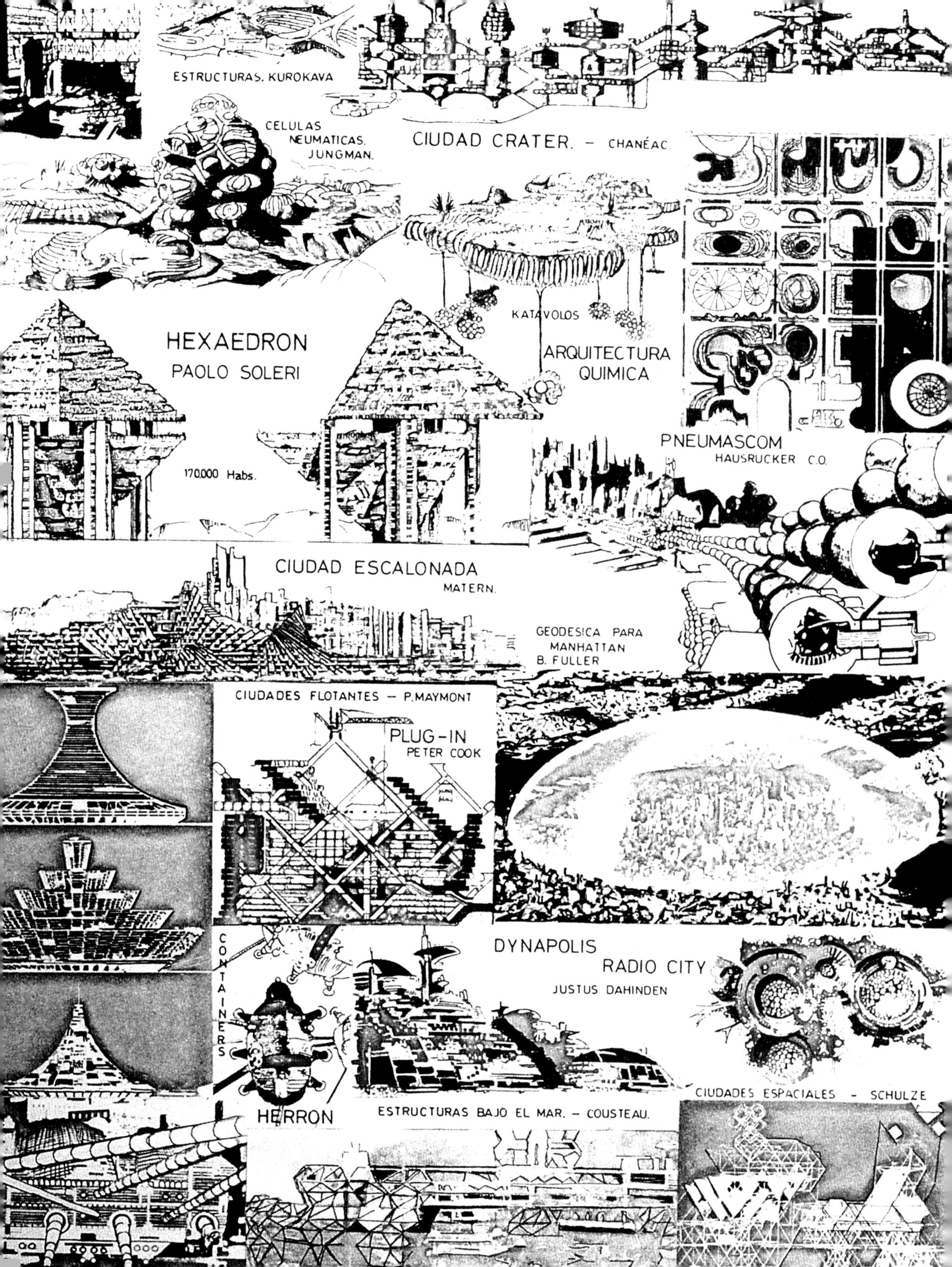
ESTRUCTURAS. KUROKAVA
CELULAS NEUMATICAS. JUNGMAN.
CIUDAD CRATER. – CHANÉAC.
HEXAEDRON
PAOLO SOLERI
170.000 Habs.
KATAVOLOS
ARQUITECTURA QUIMICA
PNEUMASCOM
HAUSRUCKER C.O.
CIUDAD ESCALONADA
MATERN.
GEODESICA PARA MANHATTAN
B. FULLER
CIUDADES FLOTANTES – P. MAYMONT
PLUG-IN
PETER COOK
CONTAINERS
DYNAPOLIS
RADIO CITY
JUSTUS DAHINDEN
CIUDADES ESPACIALES – SCHULZE
HERRON
ESTRUCTURAS BAJO EL MAR. – COUSTEAU.

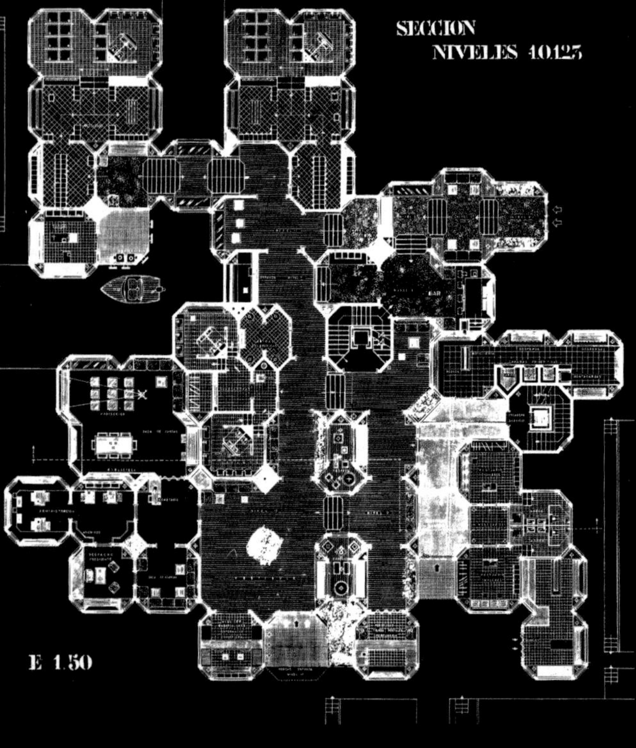


Senior thesis. "La Clota" Yatch Club. L'Escala. 1971 C. Ferrater

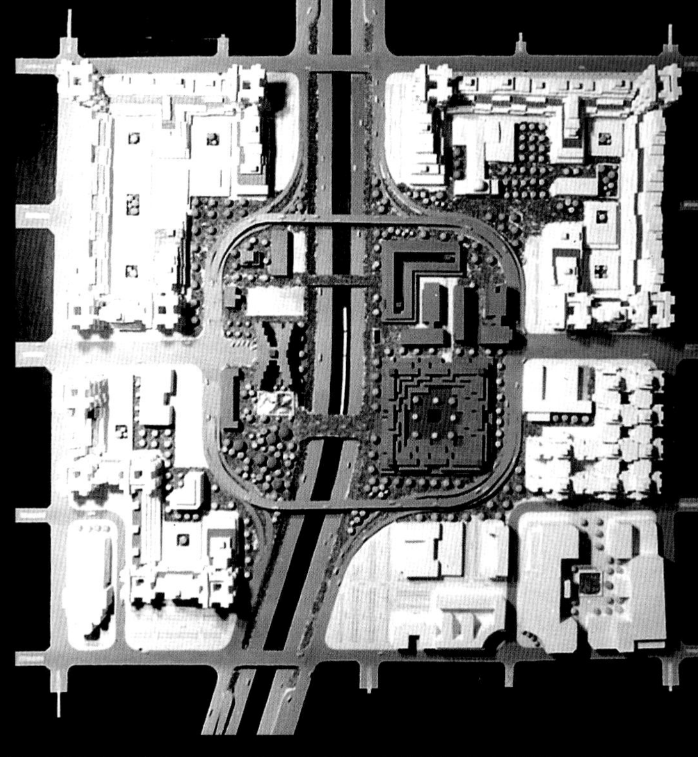

Competition in Santiago de Chile. Awarded. 1972. C. Ferrater - X. Bagué Bofill

Apartment complex in Cala Conta. Ibiza. 1972 C. Ferrater - X. Bagué Bofill

And so we reach 1971, a crucial year for me as I finished my degree and became a member of COAC. I was also able, together with Fernando Bendito and with the help of JM de Prada, to design and produce the Instant City. I set up my first studio in Carrer Riera de Sant Miquel, in a mechanical workshop. I was hired as an assistant professor by ETSAB after a year of teaching on a work experience programme and I created my first works of interest in the field of interior design. Most importantly, in October, travelling periodically to Barcelona from Ibiza, where the Instant City was growing up, self-built by its inhabitants, I was able to attend the birth of my daughter Lucía and enjoy her in the company of Inés.

At the end of 1970 I had presented my final degree project, a Sailing Club for L'Escala, on the water, in the new La Clota marina. It was marked by an examining board which could not meet, as the architecture school was closed. After collecting the reports from the different members of the examining board, I found I had obtained a B grade.

It was then that I produced my first professional works, such as the competition entry for four blocks in the centre of Santiago de Chile. Salvador Allende's government fell a few weeks after it was delivered. Years later, Emilio Donato published it in the college magazine Quaderns. Other projects that year were the Cala Comte apartment complex on Ibiza and a proposal for a contemporary Mediterranean village in Javea.

Years later, Antonio Pizza collected some of these projects in the exhibition "Architectures without Place" held at the Santa Monica Art Centre in Barcelona. At this stage I did some interior design projects, such as the interior of Tapicerías Rabanal in Avenida Diagonal, which was a finalist for the FAD awards the following year, in 1973.

First studio in Riera Sant Miquel, Barcelona, 1970

# Instant City 1971

Image by Itziar Anibarro

**José Miguel de Prada & Carlos Ferrater**

Inflatable prototype made in 48 hours on the grounds of the Aiscondel Cerdanyola factory in order to demonstrate the viability of the Instant City proposal and validate its sponsorship consisting of supplying the PVC sheet for the construction of the city free of charge.

DOMINGO, 31 DE OCTUBRE 1971 — LA VANGUARDIA ESPAÑOLA — Página 13

*Accesos a la Ciudad Instantánea ideados por los estudiantes del modo más económico y siempre con una absoluta realización manual*

# La ciudad instantánea de Ibiza

## LA CONSTRUCCION FUE CONSIDERADA COMO EXPRESIVA EXPERIENCIA DE LAS RELACIONES HUMANAS

En el mes de febrero, y en el curso de una reunión de trabajo en un estudio de arquitectura, nos planteamos la posibilidad de una articulación con ADI-FAD, la elaboración de un manifiesto y la incidencia en el Congreso Internacional de Diseño Industrial "ICSID 1971 Ibiza", que debía celebrarse a mediados del mes de octubre.

Se trataba, en principio, de hacer posible una experiencia colectiva en la que el trabajo y la información fueran los únicos canales de expresión a través de los cuales materializar una ciudad efímera que patentizara las contradicciones en las que se mueve la panorámica actual del diseño industrial.

En el mes de abril celebramos unas reuniones con ADI-FAD y posteriormente con miembros del ICSID en Ibiza, comprometiéndonos a facilitar un alojamiento a los estudiantes de diseño que quisieran asistir al Congreso.

Elaboramos un manifiesto informativo y un cartel, difundiéndolos en círculos relacionados con el diseño industrial de todo el mundo.

En posteriores sesiones de trabajo, se ejecutó un mínimo plan ordenador y se verificaron estudios con diferentes tipos de materiales: lonas, plásticos, paneles... A partir de ellos, y vista la inviabilidad del uso de diferentes materiales, se eligió un material único: film de PVC, y un único sistema constructivo: el hinchable.

Nos pusimos en contacto con José Prada, experto en arquitectura neumática, el cual elaboró un lenguaje mínimo que permitiría a cualquier persona construirse una cobertura en un tiempo reducido con un instrumental mínimo. La energía neumática que mantendría en pie la ciudad sería común a todas las células.

Disponíamos, pues, de un sistema constructivo muy tecnológico, pero para cuya realización se requerían unos métodos totalmente artesanales (grapas cada centímetro, intersecciones entre cilindros y esferas ejecutadas con cuerdas para absorber las tensiones, puertas de forma orgánica donde el ingenio daba alternativas a la carencia de medios.

Nos pusimos en contacto con las firmas comerciales que podían suministrarnos el PVC, ventiladores, grapas... Y, por fin, a finales del mes de agosto, un grupo muy reducido construimos en Sardañola el primer prototipo hinchable, y a principios de septiembre salía hacia Ibiza el primer grupo de trabajo formado por gente llegada de todo el mundo para realizar durante un mes la infraestructura necesaria y las zonas comunes.

Los primeros que fuimos y que hemos construido el espacio comunal del conjunto neumático, somos los que hemos establecido relaciones personales más sólidas. De alguna manera nos hemos sentido obreros de la misma idea. El desafío estaba planteado entre el concepto ciudad instantánea, que es un término ideológico en que por un lado se plantea el rechazo a la ciudad que va diseñando y trazando el comportamiento de sus habitantes, y por otro lado el despertar de una nueva conciencia que reclama el ocio como producto de la tecnología actual para convertirlo en el trabajo específico de la naturaleza humana, que es la creación.

Es difícil enmarcar este cuadro de ideas dentro de las posibilidades del experimento de Ibiza. La sobreestructura de congreso englobando cualquier tipo de manifestación y generando continuamente unas interrelaciones de dependencia no en exceso definidas, desvirtuaba la validez de la experiencia.

Durante el Congreso la ciudad instantánea se convirtió en plataforma publicitaria, miles de fotografías y kilómetros de película, el espacio construido adquiere un significado escultórico formal.

Queda, sin embargo, como interrogante a los visitantes y tema de conversación para los congresistas el inmenso trabajo acumulado (650 000 grapas cosidas manualmente), así como la contradicción de un espacio futurista y la suciedad y desorden interior. Pero una vez dentro, la sensación del espacio escapa a la habitual percepción y los sentidos se ven alterados, la sobrepresión, principio invisible, crea un determinado desconcierto mágico que se convierte en admiración de lo elemental.

La ciudad instantánea es la primera experiencia nacional en la que se ha intentado plantear la construcción como experiencia expresiva de las relaciones humanas.

Queda de ella unos miles de metros cuadrados construidos, el cascarón del gusanito que se ha marchado esperando una alternativa de uso ecológico, una serie de relaciones personales, el valor del trabajo como vehículo de comunicación y la clara conciencia del momento histórico en que vivimos. El éxito o el fracaso poco importa, lo esencial es el conocimiento.

*Fernando BENDITO*
*Carlos FERRATER*

*En primer término los hinchables de la Ciudad Instantánea, al fondo los hoteles. Obra del arquitecto Raimon Torres*

*Vista general en proceso de construcción de la red de hinchables*

IBIZA'S INSTANT CITY
Sunday, 31 October, 1971
LA VANGUARDIA

(Translation from original newspaper)

## THE INSTANT CITY OF IBIZA

The construction was considered to be an expressive experiment in human relations

In February, during a work meeting in an architecture studio, we discussed the possibility of developing a manifesto with ADI-FAD and presenting it at the International Congress of Industrial Design "ICSID 1971 Ibiza", which was to be held in mid-October.

In principle, the idea was to make possible a collective experiment in which work and information would be the only channels of expression for creating a temporary city that would show up the contradictions of the situation in industrial design at the time. In April, we held meetings with ADI-FAD and, later, with members of ICSID in Ibiza, committing ourselves to provide accommodation for design students wishing to attend the Congress. We developed a manifesto to provide information and a poster, distributing them in circles related to industrial design around the world.

In subsequent work sessions, a minimal organisational plan was drawn up and studies were carried out with different types of materials: tarpaulins, plastics, panels, and so on. Based on these, and considering the unfeasibility of using a combination of materials, a single material – PVC film – and a single construction system – the inflatable – were chosen.

We contacted José Prada, an expert in inflatable architecture, who drew up a minimal language that would allow anyone to build a pneumatic covering in a short time with the minimum tools. The pneumatic energy to keep the city standing would be common to all cells. We therefore had a highly technological construction system that required absolutely traditional methods (staples every centimetre, intersections between cylinders and spheres achieved with ropes to absorb the tensions, and organic doors for which ingenuity provided alternatives to the lack of resources).

We contacted the commercial firms that could supply us with PVC, fans, staples and so on. And finally, at the end of August, a very small group of us built the first inflatable prototype at Cerdanyola, and, at the beginning of September, the first working group, consisting of people from all over the world, left for Ibiza to build the necessary infrastructure and communal areas. This took a month. Those of us who were the first to build the communal space of the inflatable complex are the ones who have established the strongest personal relationships.

Somehow, we felt like workers striving for the same idea. The challenge concerned the concept of the instant city, which is an ideological term that suggests, on one hand, the rejection of a city that designs and marks out its inhabitants' behaviour and, on the other, awakening a new consciousness to champion leisure as a product of modern technology to make it into work specific to human nature, which is creating things. It is difficult to frame these ideas within the possibilities of the Ibiza experiment. The superstructure of the congress, encompassing any type of manifestation and continually generating relationships of dependency that were not all that well defined, distorted the validity of the experiment.

During the Congress, the instant city became an advertising platform: thousands of photographs were taken and kilometres of film were exposed on it, and the built space took on a formal, sculptural meaning. However, the tremendous amount of work done (650,000 staples manually inserted) remains as a curiosity for visitors and a topic of conversation for congress participants.

There was also the contradiction of such a futuristic space with all that dirt and disorder inside it. But, once inside, the sensation of space escaped the usual perception and the senses were altered. The invisible excess pressure created a degree of magical bewilderment that turned into admiration for the elemental.

The instant city is the first experiment in Spain in which the intention has been to approach construction as an expressive experiment in human relations.

What remains of it are a few thousand square metres built – the shell of the little worm that has left us, awaiting an alternative ecological use; a series of personal relationships; the value of work as a vehicle for communication; and a clear awareness of the historical moment in which we live. Success or failure matter little: the essential thing is knowledge.

Fernando Bendito – Carlos Ferrater

Instant City photos by José Manuel Ferrater

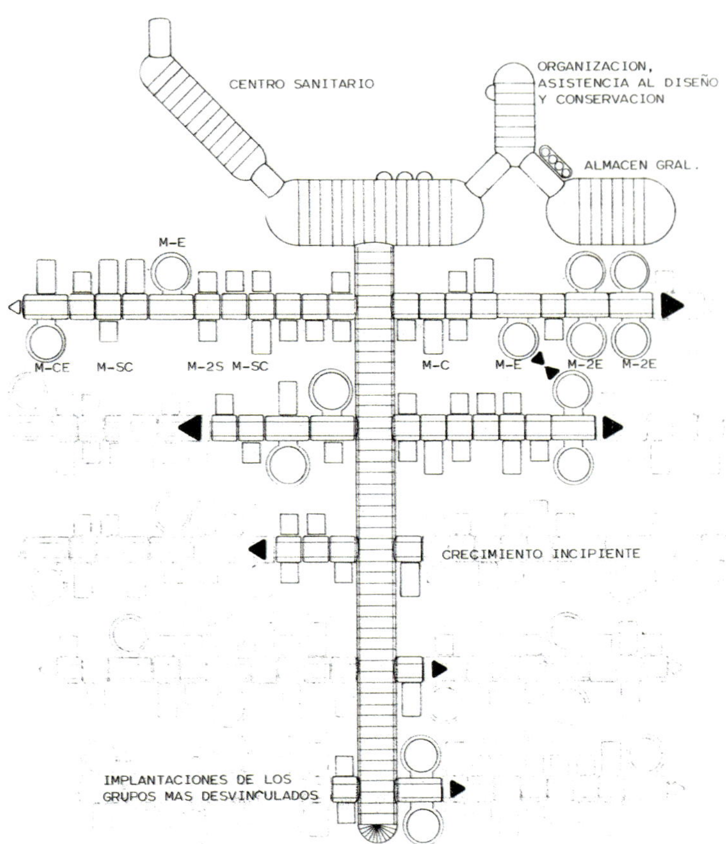


Poster. J.M. Ferrater

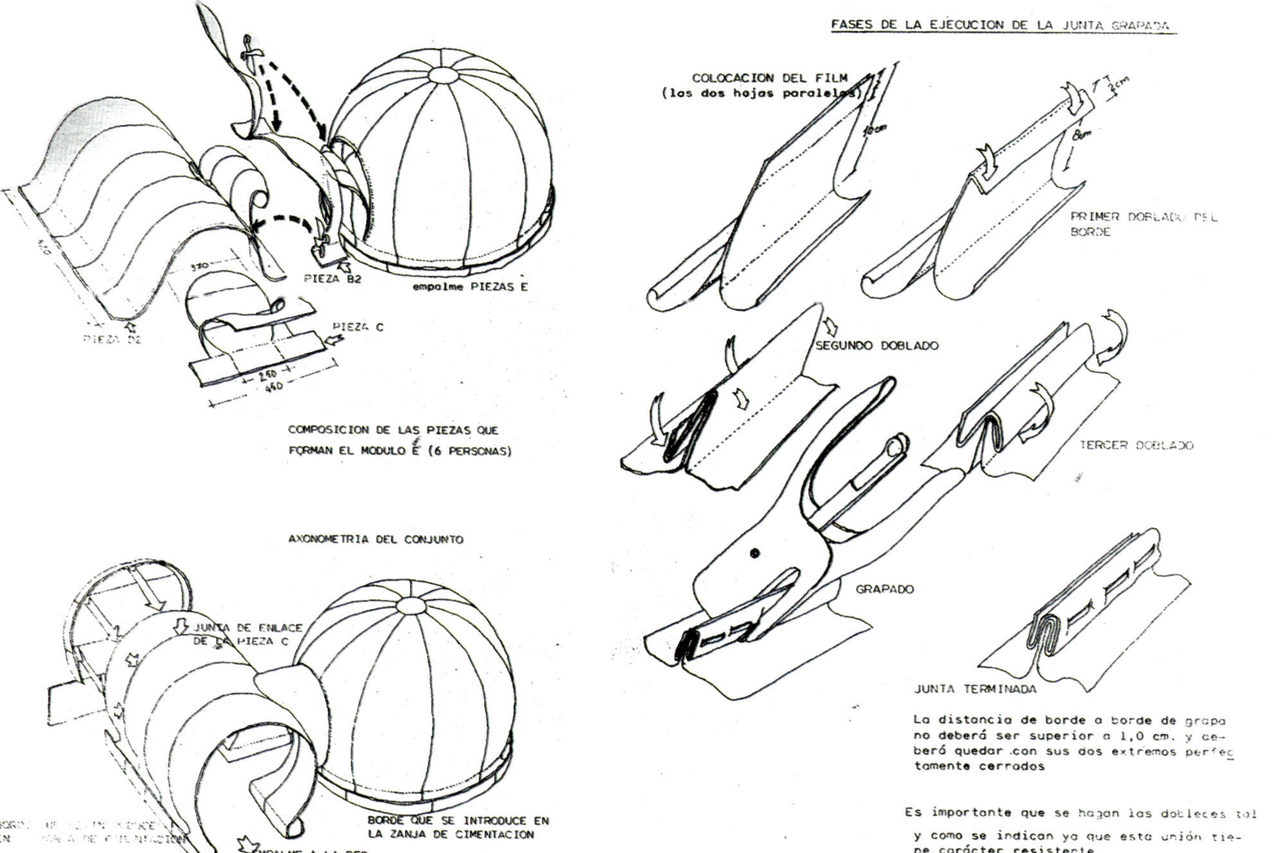


Ensambling Instructions J.M. de Prada-Poole

The community. The individual

## INSTANT CITY

La CIUDAD INSTANTANEA es una llamada a la imaginación y un experimento de vida en comunidad. Se creará la CIUDAD INSTANTANEA coincidiendo con el Congreso del ICSID que se celebrará en IBIZA del 13 al 17 de octubre de 1971. Nos han cedido unos 15.000m². de terreno al lado del mar y de los hoteles en Cala San Miguel.

Se construirá una infraestructura mínima, redes de energía, gabinete de información y centro asesor del diseño, de los días 5 al 20 de septiembre y, a partir del 21 cada uno podrá edificar su módulo de habitación y entre todos diseñar y construir zonas, circulaciones y espacios comunes. Para ello se dispondrá de 15.000m² de cloruro de polivinilo de diferentes colores, 15.000 m. lineales de cinta adhesiva, y el instrumental necesario y manual de instrucciones técnicas destinado a facilitar el diseño y construcción de esta 1ª ciudad neumática del mundo

Esperamos que la vida en comunidad facilitará todo tipo de manifestaciones artísticas espontáneas, sobre todo si tenemos en cuenta que vendrán a vivir con nosotros grupos de teatro, música, mimo. La vida en la ciudad será un espectáculo total, los habitantes de la ciudad podrán realizar experiencias de cualquier tipo sin necesidad de establecer un programa previo.

No existe programación alguna, los únicos canales de comunicación previstos serán la información por murales, pregones o periódicos y el trabajo.

Hemos pensado establecer un gran economato donde, en el peor de los casos, se puedan comprar alimentos a precio de coste; no obstante, nuestro propósito sería poder dar gratis ciertos alimentos básicos tales como pan, arroz, frutos secos, hortalizas, etc..Desgraciadamente hasta ahora contamos sólo con una pequeña subvención. Cualquier ayuda, idea, o iniciativa particular ayudará a resover este problema. Hay que considerar que la CIUDAD INSTANTANEA es, principalmente, una idea compartida. Nosotros desde Barcelona desearíamos limitarnos a ser una comisión coordinadora, y que, La Ciudad fuera un fruto de todos nosotros.

La inscripción es libre, solamente se trata de que nos avisen el día de llegada. Tenemos pensado reservar 20 plazas en el barco diario que sale desde Barcelona, por lo que insistimos en saber de antemano la fecha de su llegada. Es interesante saber que también salen barcos desde Valencia y Alicante. Recomendamos que cada persona se traiga consigo un saco de dormir y los utensilios de comida.

Esperamos, pues, sus noticias diciéndonos con exactitud la fecha de llegada. En Ibiza una comisión estará esperando a los que vengan. Esperando una pequeña ayuda para los amigos, deseamos paz,

Comité Ad Hoc para la Ciudad
Instantánea
ADI/FAD
c. Brusi, 39. BARCELONA (6)
ESPAÑA.

Individually sharing the air of the city

Tribute tricorn

# IBIZA: UN WOODS-TOCK EN EL QUE EL DISEÑO SUSTITUYO A LA FUNCION UNIFICADORA DE LA MUSICA

Los festivales de música, Woodstock, fueron en su día una manifestación colectiva de una cultura. Este verano, o mejor este otoño, ha habido entre nosotros algo que bien pudiera ser un equivalente de tales manifestaciones. En este caso, el elemento conglomerante no ha sido la música, a pesar de haber habido músicos y música, sino el diseño y el trabajo colectivo de un grupo de cien personas que durante un mes construyeron una ciudad efímera en la cala de San Miguel, de Ibiza. La Instant City. Se trataba, en principio, de que un congreso de diseño posibilitara una experiencia colectiva en la que el trabajo y la información fueran los únicos canales de expresión a través de los cuales materializar una ciudad instantánea que patentizara las contradicciones en las que se mueve la panorámica actual del diseño y que ofreciera una posibilidad más de acorde con las necesidades de la nueva cultura. El resultado fueron una serie de jóvenes arquitectos, músicos, artesanos, grupos de teatro, gente interesada en el experimento trabajando juntos en la construcción de una gigantesca vivienda neumática multicolor multiceludar. El trabajo en común, el trabajo hecho experimentación, creatividad y juego dio como fruto una convivencia de agradables vibraciones, de serenidad. El ambiente físico creado al vivir dentro de plástico de colores proporcionó una alteración de sentidos, un ambiente especial creado por la sobrepresión, por el aire procedente de los ventiladores que sustentaban la presión necesaria del hinchable, la atmósfera extrañamente húmeda del plástico... Los grupos de música y de teatro que habían acudido a la ciudad no actuaban, vivían, convivían y trabajaban en el experimento. Llegó el congreso oficial, llegó la cultura tradicional, se intentó compatibilizarlas en una fiesta de inauguración común. Frank Miralda, organizador de fiestas en Francia, organizador de la fiesta azul de Paco Rabanne, organizó el show..., una comida de colores. Pero la comunicación no se logró, se produjo el choque y la fiesta terminó en basura. De ahí surgió un espectáculo teatral. Cada uno se expresa con los medios de que dispone, y el grupo de teatro argentino, que hasta entonces había estado trabajando, inició actuaciones de protesta y lamento ante la incomunicación, en los comedores de los hoteles en que se desarrollaba el congreso oficial. Pero las vibraciones habían cambiado ya. En uno de los últimos días hubo algo que volvió a subir el viaje, una actuación de Pau Riba, la única actuación organizada de la ciudad. Ibiza no fue Woodstock, pero Ibiza ha marcado el primer paso de una trayectoria. Se habla de una nueva ciudad efímera, quizás en Almería, quizá de fibra de vidrio, quizá de cartones impermeabilizados. ¿Serán para nosotros los arquitectos y no los músicos los que nos traigan la nueva cultura? ¿O quizás ambos? ¿O quizá todos? De la Instant City de Ibiza queda el cascarón de un gusanito de plástico que los payeses de Ibiza van a recortar por las noches para utilizarlo domésticamente, un gusanito multicolor que se ha marchado después de ser la casa de unos centenares de jóvenes durante un mes.

María-José RAGUE ARIAS

Parallel performances during the Instant City in Ibiza. 1971

01

02

03

04

05

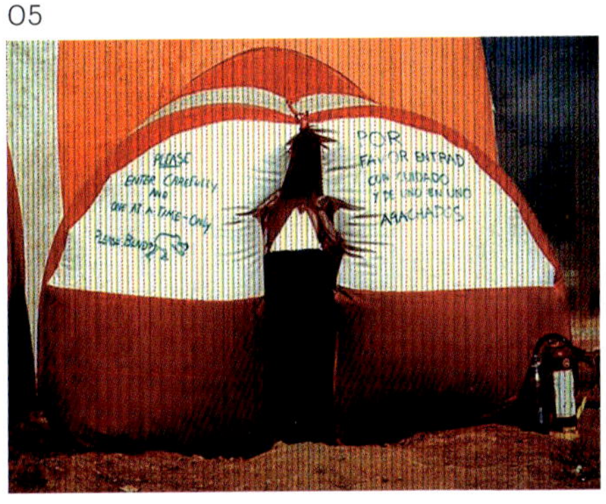


06

07

08

09

10

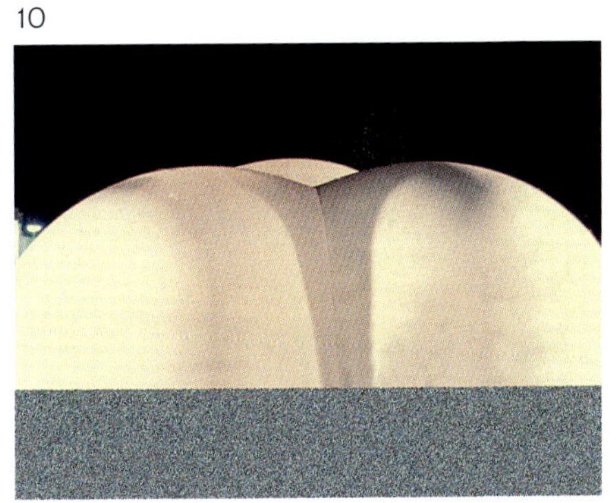

As the first inhabitants arrived in mid-September from California, South America, northern and central Europe, and even Japan (1), the first work teams were organised at the initial assembly, together with the cooperative to take care of the city's food supply (2). These teams were in charge of building the large communal inflatable, the main corridor (3) and the first living quarters (4), following JM de Prada's instructions.

Privacy was at a premium and communal life caused problems of coexistence due to the misuse of community facilities and accesses, so the first rules, recommendations and prohibitions appeared (5). These resulted in the first desertions. A group of dissatisfied inhabitants decided to move to the northern slope of the cove, building their communal home with reeds and the remains of the film used to construct the city (6).

In mid-October some local people arrived to study how they could recycle the material used for construction. For years the north of the island was dotted with multi-coloured coverings for haystacks, agricultural facilities, tractors and machinery (7). Meanwhile, after the instant city disappeared, Cala Sant Miquel returned to its original state (8).

Fernando Bendito travelled to India where he stayed for several years and, after the promotional success we had achieved, Aiscondel offered me the chance to carry on designing and building pneumatic structures.

Together with Marià Pedrol, who had accompanied us from the beginning, I was able to build several inflatables, including the one at Benidorm to promote the new town (9), as well as the Aiscondel Pavilion at the Feria del Campo in Madrid, with a sophisticated pattern of spheres and truncated cones that won the Silver Medal at the event.

Carlos Ferrater

# L' Estartit. Costa Brava 1979-1991

Until a few years ago L'Estartit was a modest village spread out in a line along a narrow strip of land between beach and mountain. The appearance of L'Estartit was that of a typical fishing village of small row houses, their alignment set back where geography required it, forming an ensemble of whitewashed dwellings against the green backdrop of the mountain.

A harbor wall was constructed with its own Promenade, thus creating a large marina in place of the former beach.

In the 1940s, when the Arquer family decided to spend their summers in L'Estartit, the few inhabitants, mostly Protestant fishermen, were obsessed by the idea that the Church would not allow them to be buried in the Catholic cemetery.

01. Port Building 02. Guix de la Meda 03. Garbí Building 04. Casa Molinet 05. Cap de la Barra 06. Sailing Club

Motores Marinos
VOLVO PENTA
Rio
GLASTRON
mistral m
NAUTIC

ZONA

## Guix de la Meda 1984

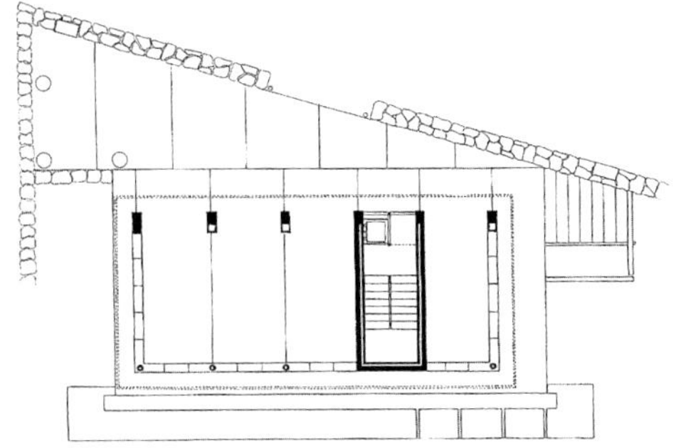

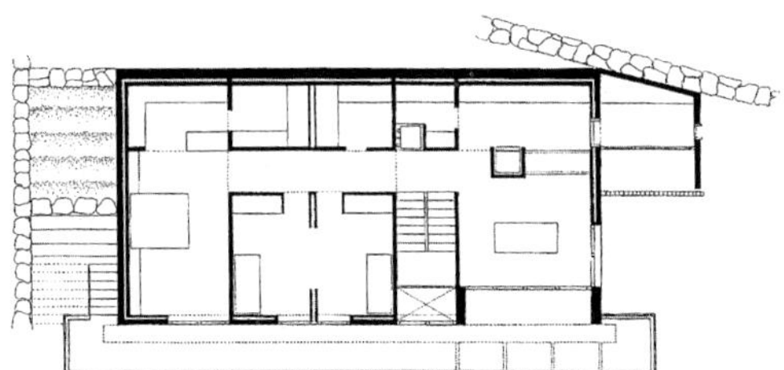

Not often is one faced with designing a single-family home on a site with such a pronounced landscape and characteristics.

This house is located on the north side of the l'Estartit Bay facing east towards the Medas Islands. The site dominates 'el freu' and is protected by a cliff from the north wind. A road at the top to the property provides access to the site.

Facing the house is a small bright triangular island used as navigational reference point, calles 'el Guix de la Meda'.

The small copper and glass triangular roof that covers the entrance to the house derives its form from this island.

In section the project was conceived of in response to the sharp level changes of the site. At the geometric center of the project terraced platforms containing the swimming pool and an outdoor dining area are located.

This is a house dug into the hill, designed based on the section because the rock behind is vertical to create platforms in the geometric centre for terraces, a swimming pool, an arbour and other features.

Seen from the sea, the house can be understood as a superimposition of wall planes rising from the rustic masonry, through cypress hedge walls, walls clad with stone slabs, walls of wooden planks, and handmade brick walls, until the upper layer is reached with its concrete canopies and the small copper roof.

Inside, a small lift and a staircase go up through the different areas of the house. Outside, a staircase at one end connects the two levels of bedrooms.

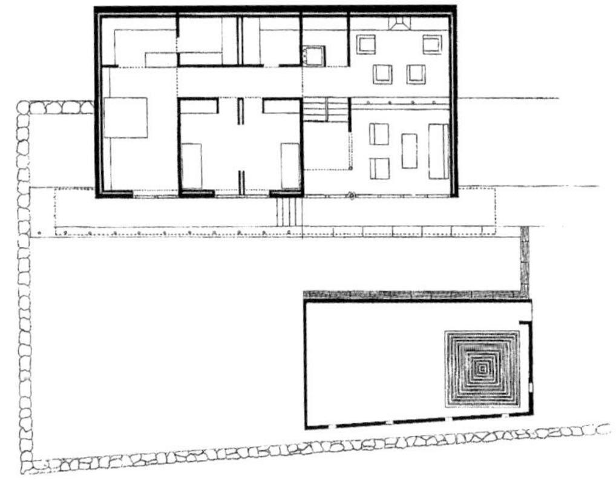

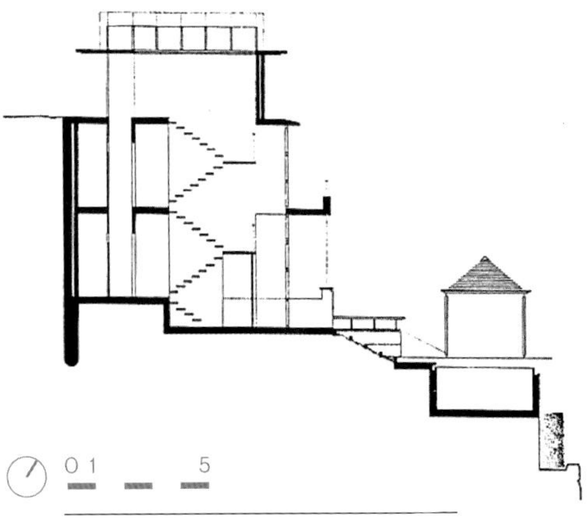

0 1 5

Floor Plans and cross section

casa

SANDRA

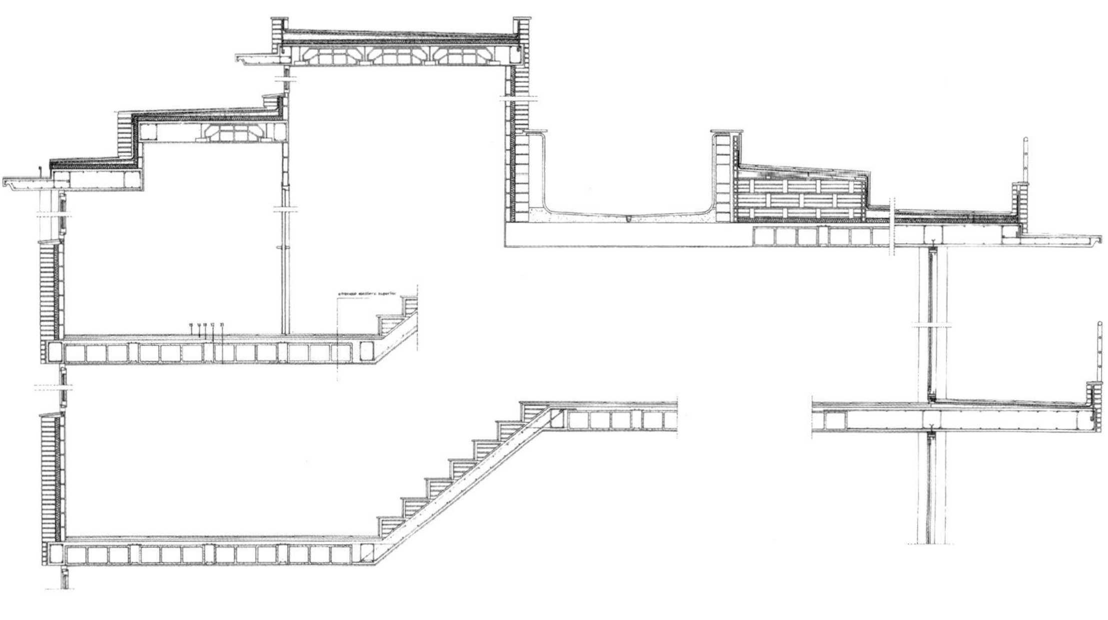

Detail section

## Molinet House 1986-1988
## L'Estartit. Girona

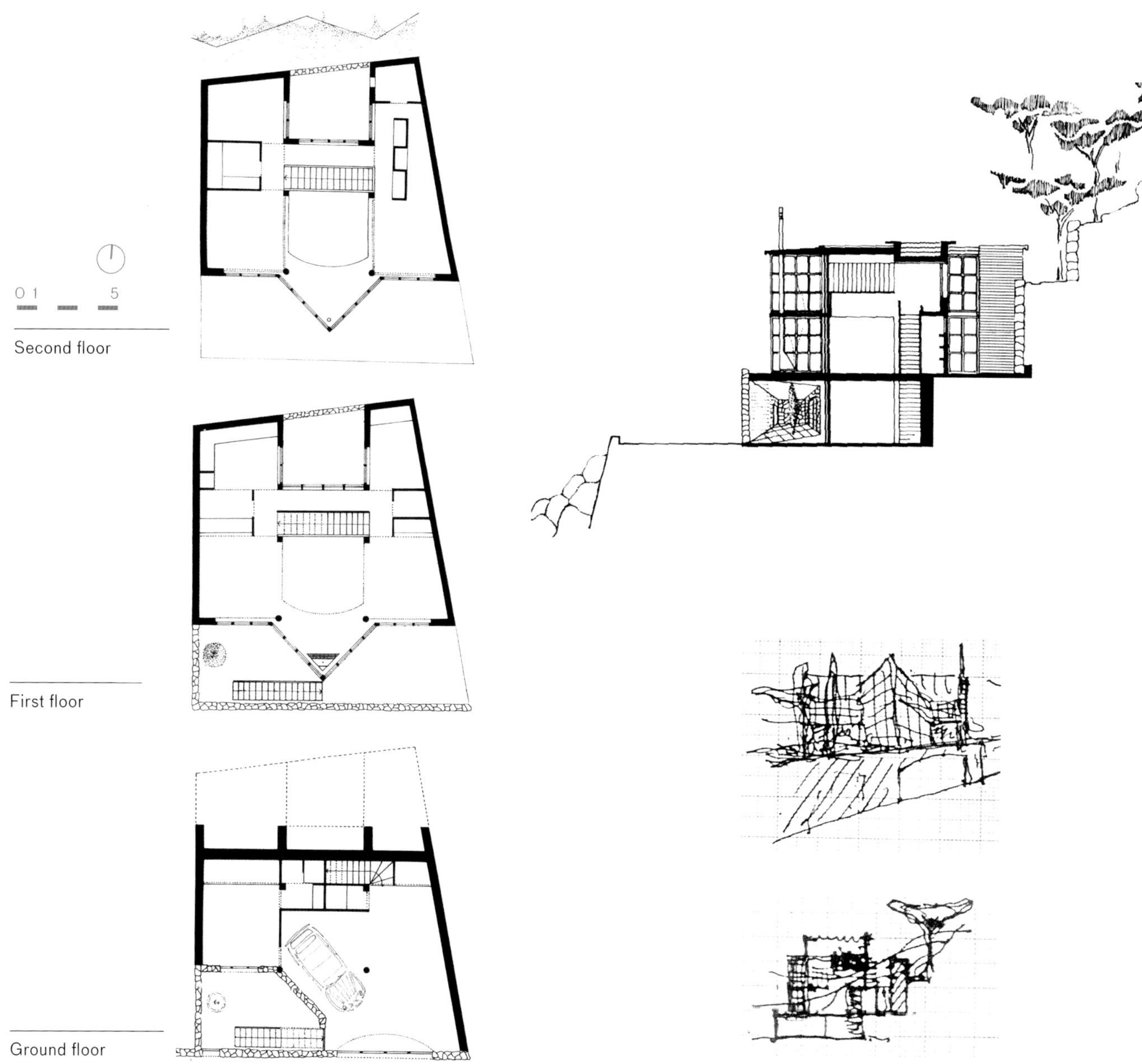


From a height of three meters above the sea level, the Passeig del Molinet follows the rocky shoreline, extending from the pier that closes l'Estartit basin to the Molinet, a crag that controls the 'freu', a channel of water between the island and the coast.

Behind a stone wall, an exterior teak stair connects the paved courtyard to the upper terrace, with access to the guestroom. These rooms are reconstructed over the old walls and open directly to the patio. A door beneath the stair leads to the garage. A second transversal stair leads to the floors above, dividing the house by separating the service areas from the living areas.

The project was conceived in terms of the section.

A double height space is created by the large central void with usual connections to the hill and the rear garden by an arched window overlooking the patio and to the ocean by a large prow-like window that encloses the main façade.

Image by Lourdes Jansana

Construction details notebook

This site notebook shows a selection of drawings and design details made on site associated with the pacts and agreements signed between the different representatives of the tradespeople and manufacturers and the project managers who directed the work.

The purpose of these agreements was to see that the initial general budget of a project in which no single construction company was responsible for the building was not altered.

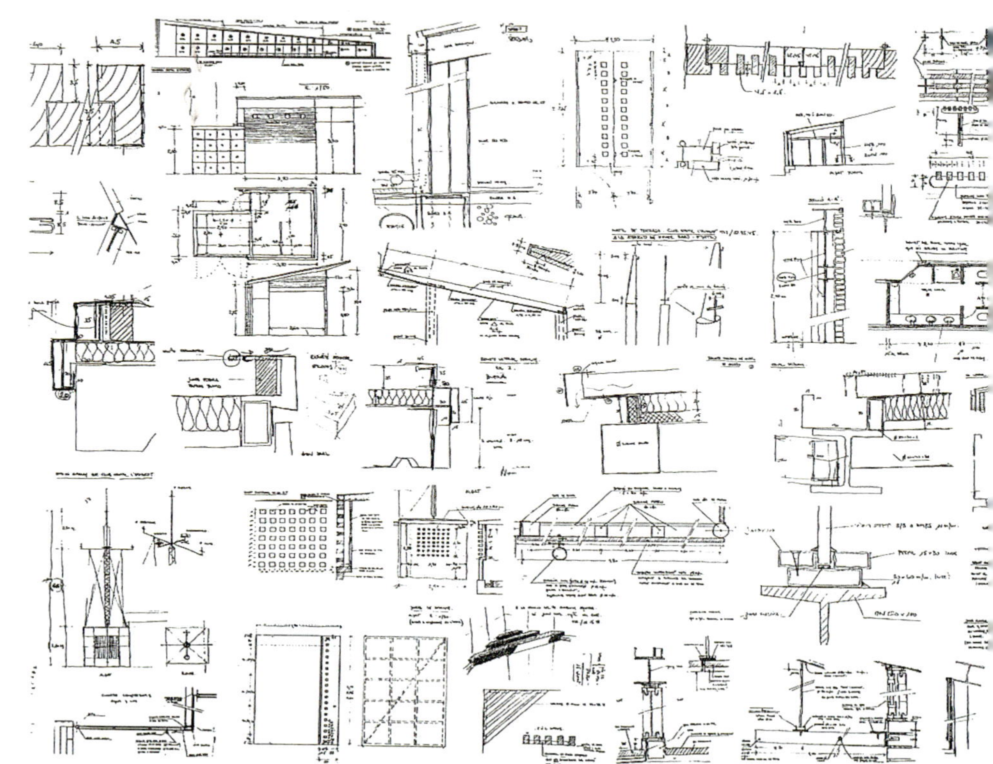

Axonometric view

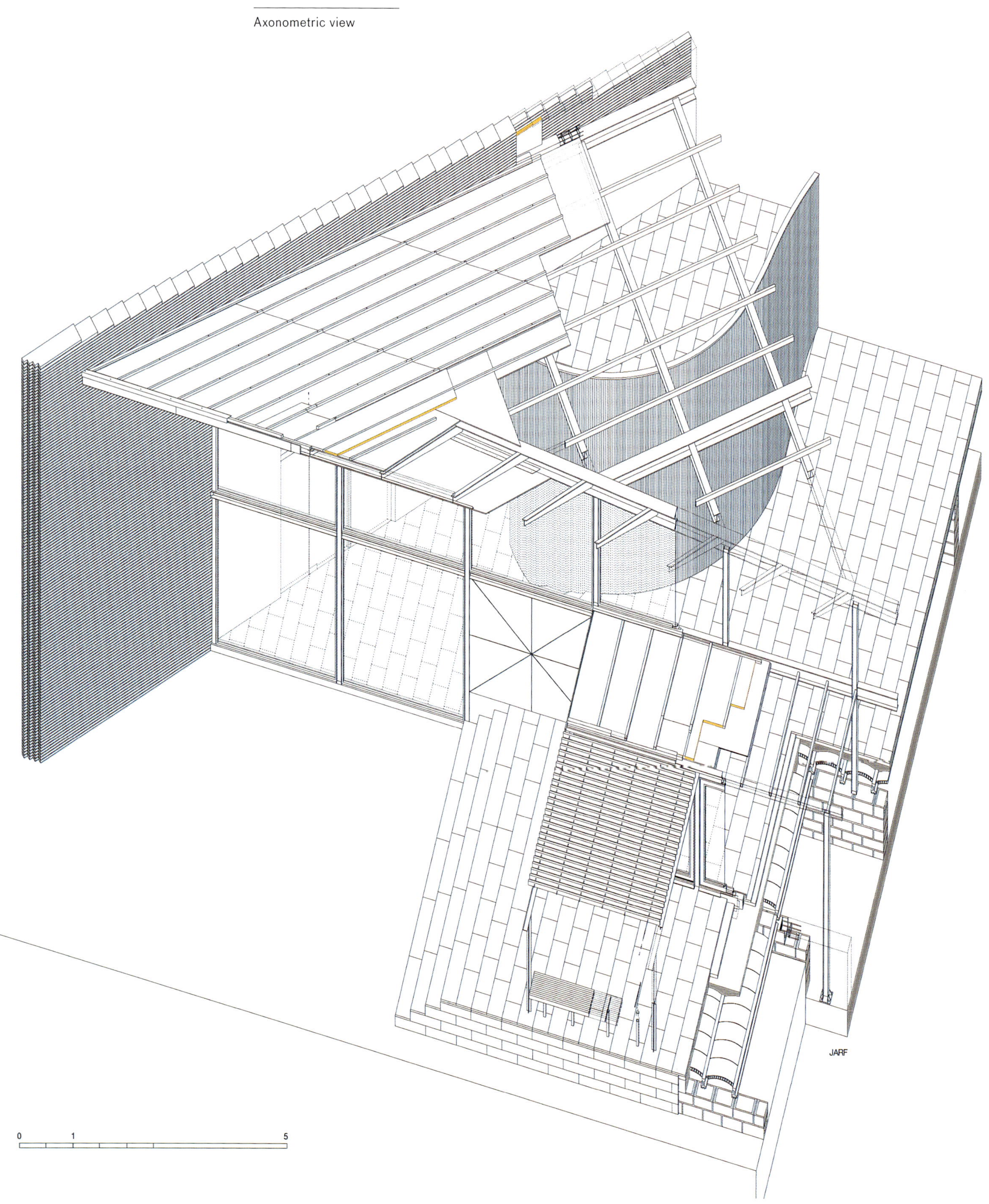

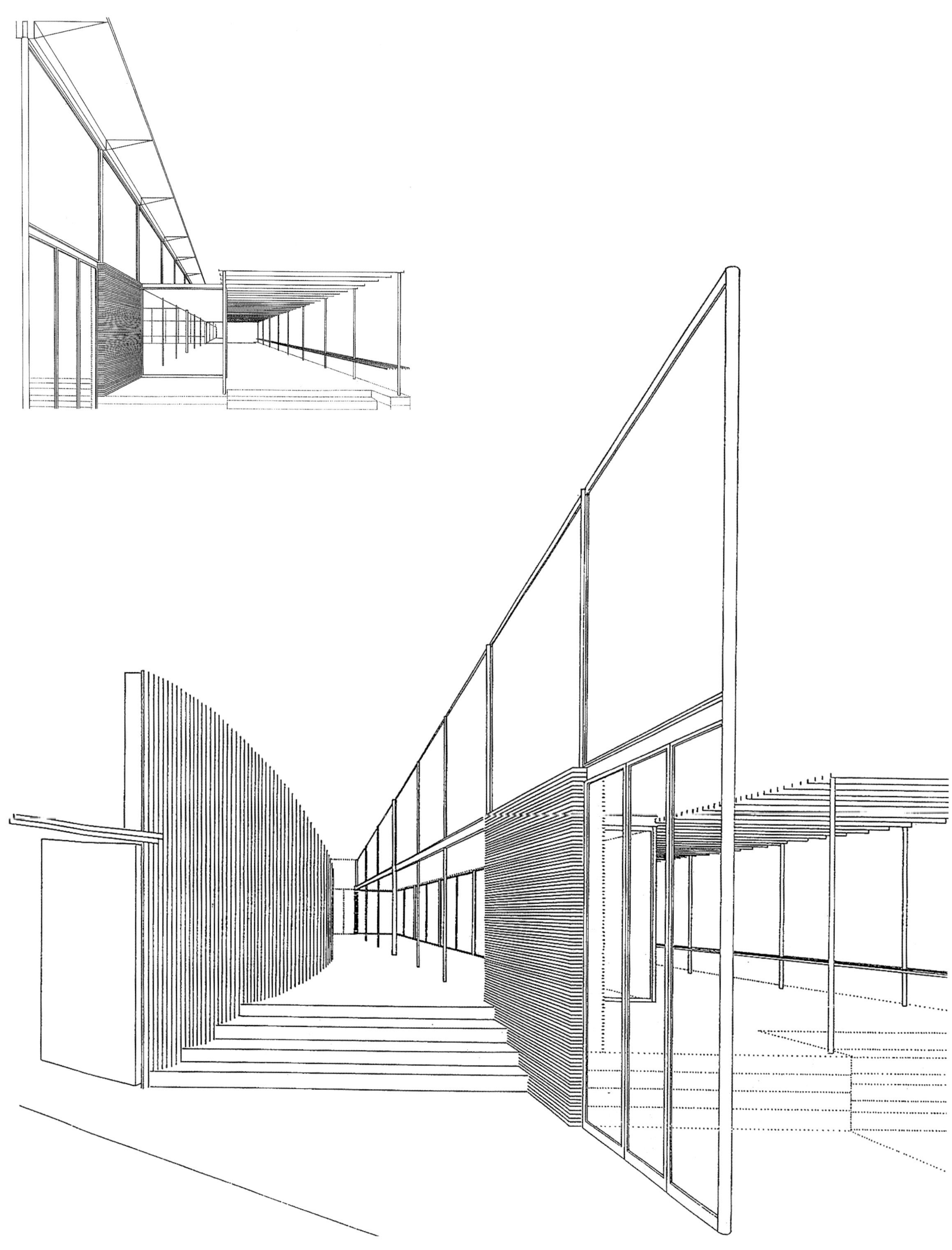

# Sant Just 1972-1985

## Sant Just Park 1972-1975

The project consisted of locating a residential complex in a landscaped estate with a steep slope, located on the outskirts of Barcelona. The previous step consisted of arranging some volumes in the section of the land, preserving the tree masses.

Analyzing today the project carried out at the beginning of the seventies, he observed how those staggered buildings against the slope of the mountain, which were designed with an eye on Coderch, for me the last great master, and which were built with manual brick, melis wood and black iron chimneys that rise up between the pines, withstand the passage of time well.

The plants, which have been covering the stepped facades as an extension of the garden, together with the nobility of the materials used, have contributed to this good permanence over time.

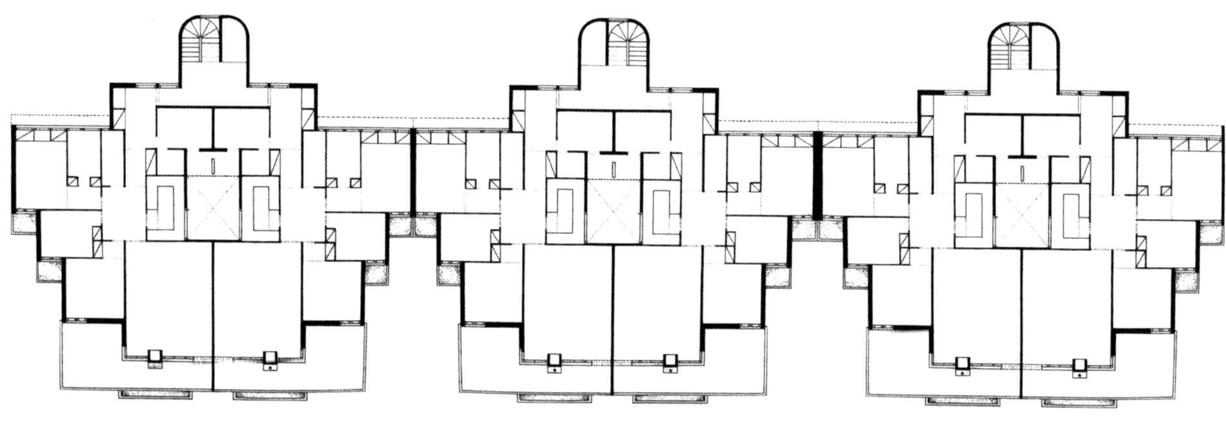

Ground Floor A1, A2 & A3

0 1 10

Ground Floor B1 & B2

Image by Carlos Ferrater

## A trip to Finland 1985-1988

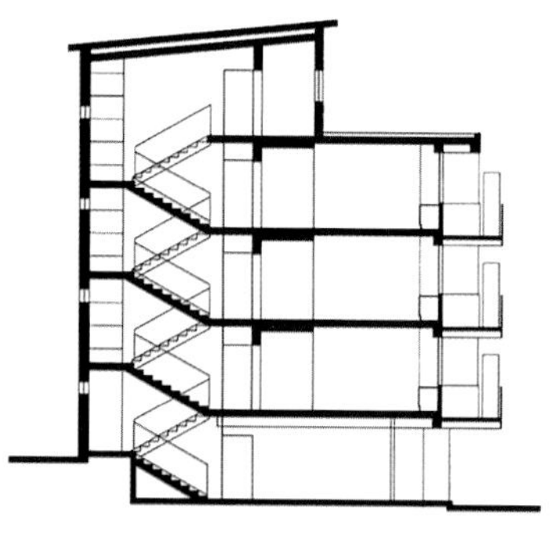

Tapiola Garden Apartment Building

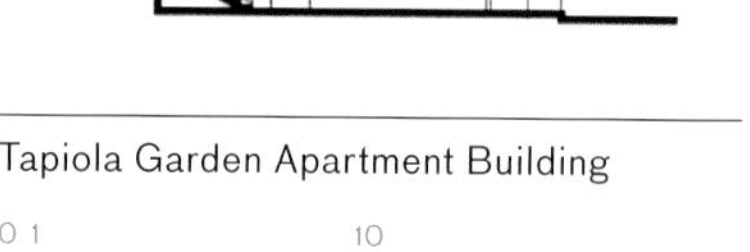


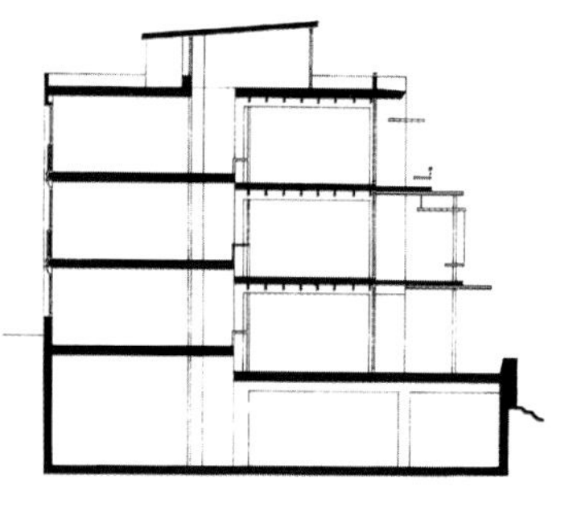

Apartment Building in a forest

After a trip to Finland, where we visited some residential areas built next to lakes and forests, we found a group of small buildings among trees in Tapiola Garden: a beautiful way of living in natural surroundings.

After a few years we decided to build our new home together with some friends in Sant Just, in a forest of pines and oaks overlooking the sea next to Sant Just Park.

On the upper part of the site, amidst a forest, close to the edge of the mountain, is a small building of three storeys and approximately 300 m2 per floor.

There are two access routes; one is a tunnel under the garden that leads to the parking lot and communal service area, the other is a small trail through the garden along a wall sided with magnolias, which leads to the cylindrical entrance.

The considerations which prevailed during the design of this project were:

– To achieve a good relationship between the houses and their context:

– The openings must adopt different solutions with respect to the function and external conditions

– The large terraces with canopies and pergolas on the south facade overlooked by the living rooms.

– The glass tower at the corner overlooking some ancient gardens.

– The opening in the form of a large window grouping the children's bedrooms over the back garden.

– The cut clean window at the end of the corridor.

All these contribute to achieve a good relation between the different areas, with their outdoor counterparts, achieving a complex organization stemming from the simplicity of the outline in plan, one in which spaces overlap with fluidity, following the order of the structure.

Also important to emphasize the construction using layers of manual brickwork, which when interrupted, allow the reading of mixed pillars and reinforced concrete decks with partial aspects such as the use of articulated rigid joints, simply loaded or with overhangs on the large front façade.

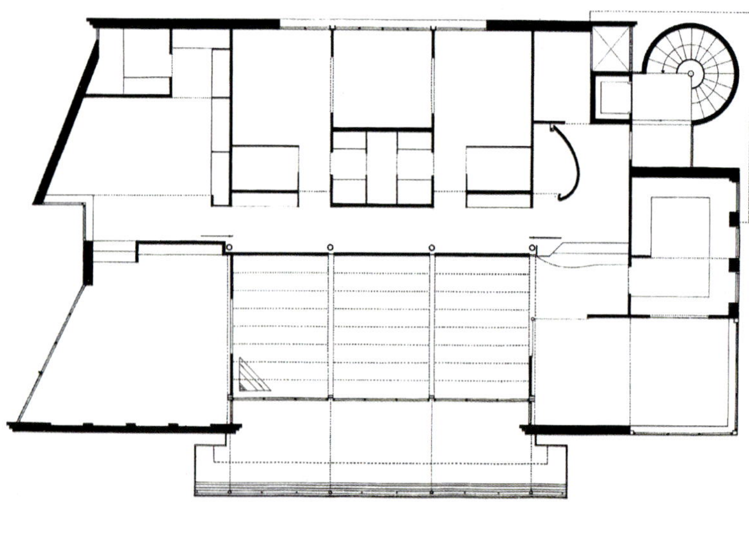

Floor plan

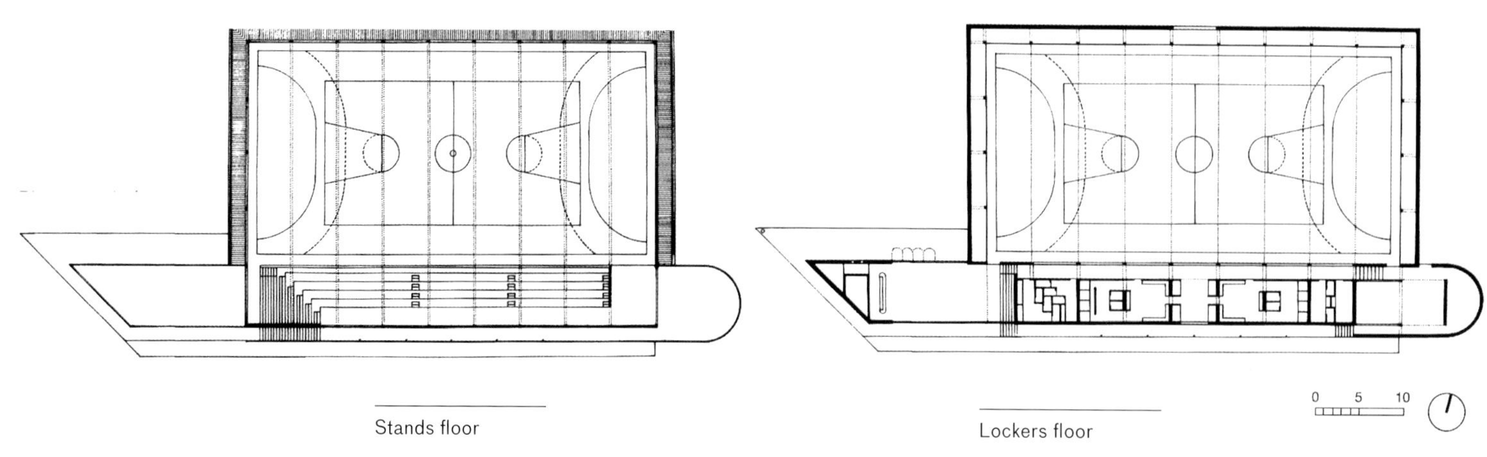
Stands floor
Lockers floor
0 5 10

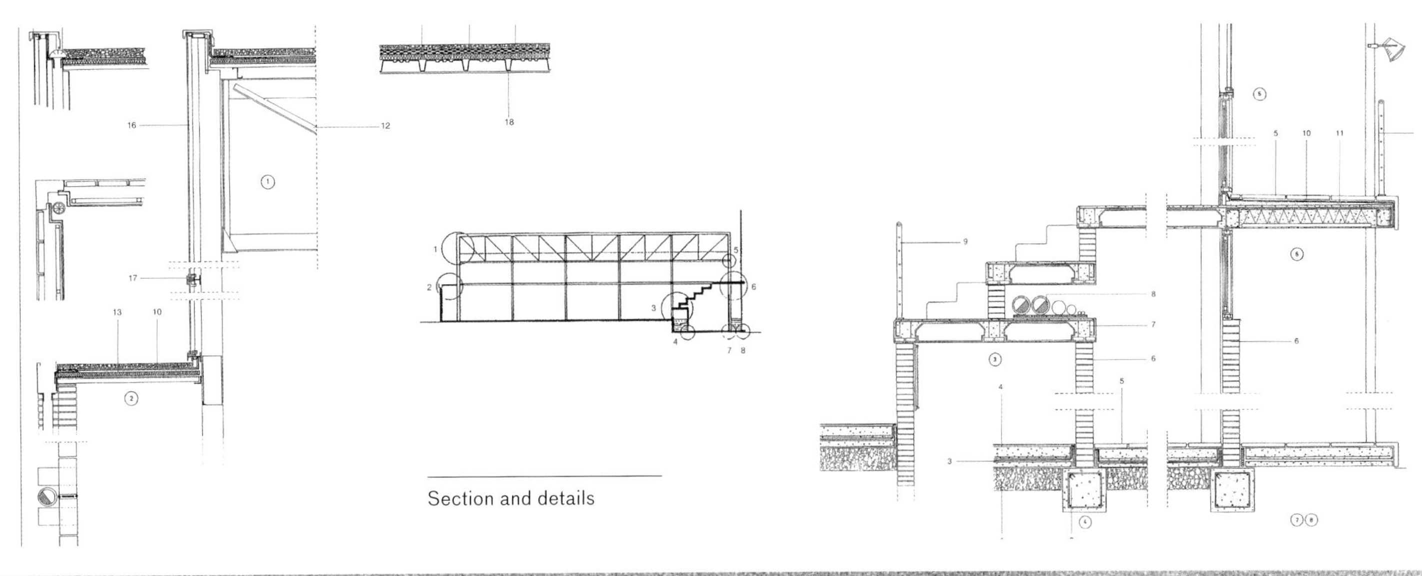

Section and details

## Torreblanca Garden
## Area Metropolitana de Barcelona 1981

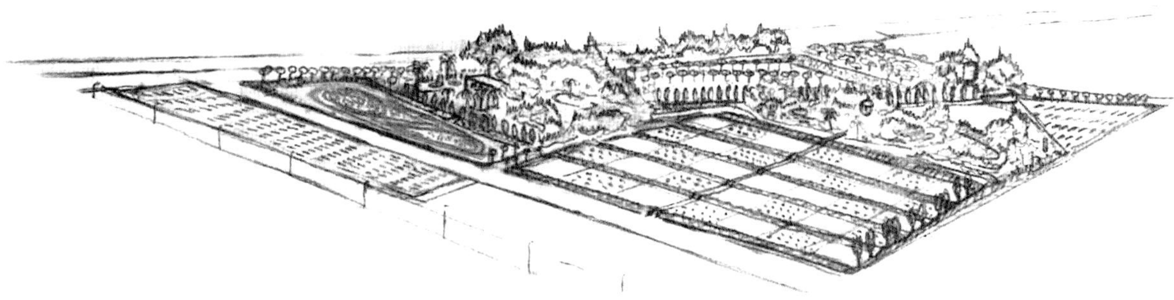

When we accepted the commission for this park project, we found ourselves confronted with the remains of some old gardens which had been laid out around a now-vanished palatial residence, a large lake with islands in it -in a state of extreme dilapidation- surrounded by magnificent trees, and the remainder of the almost 14 hectare site in use as farmland.

After careful examination of the topography, the project took the form of marking out an avenue of cypresses on a gentle gradient, facing to the east, thus knitting together the different wooded areas to make the layout of the new park a container enclosing the old gardens.

Large landscaped areas were created, in the form of extensions to the original nucleus, by the use of symmetries and geometries applied to a variety of different elements: pavilion, entrance gates, the old axes and so on.

In the competition, with entry by invitation, held by the AMB for the old gardens of the Marquises of Monistrol, in our first plan we proposed to renovate the romantic lake and the remains of the old gardens, stitching them all together with an avenue of cypress trees flanked by stone sphinxes that had been found abandoned at the southern end of the estate.

We surrounded the restored complex with large wooded areas of contemporary geometric designs, rather in the manner of a violin case.

Finally, we reconstructed the ground plan of the old palace that had disappeared as if it were a plant labyrinth, with clipped hedges.

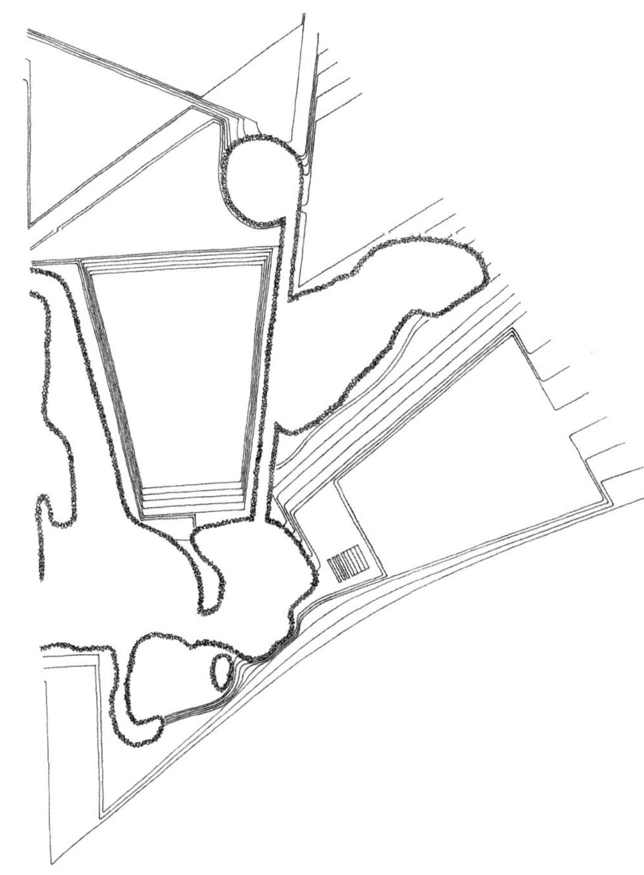

# Restoration of the ancient winery into the Consell Comarcal Baix Llobregat Headquarters. 1995

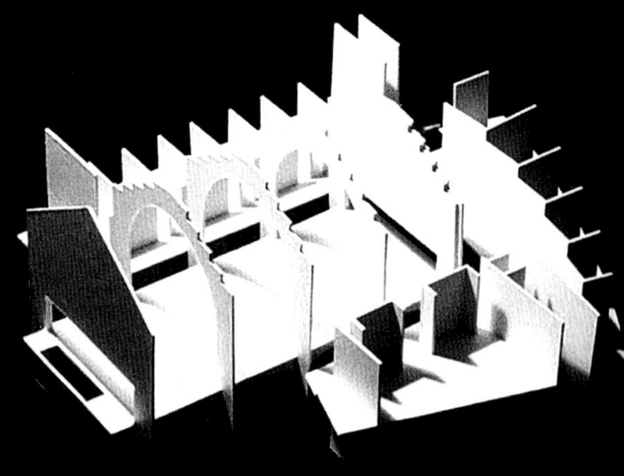

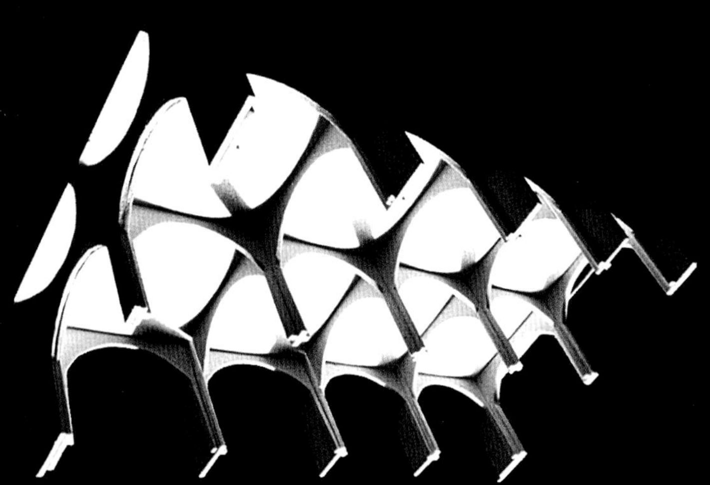

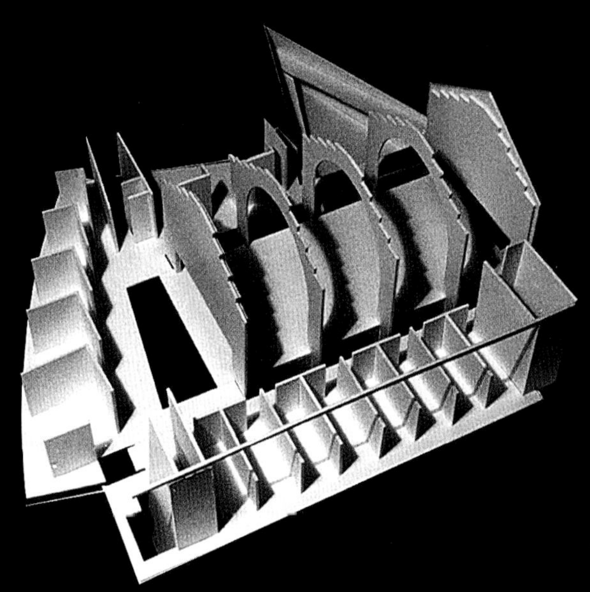

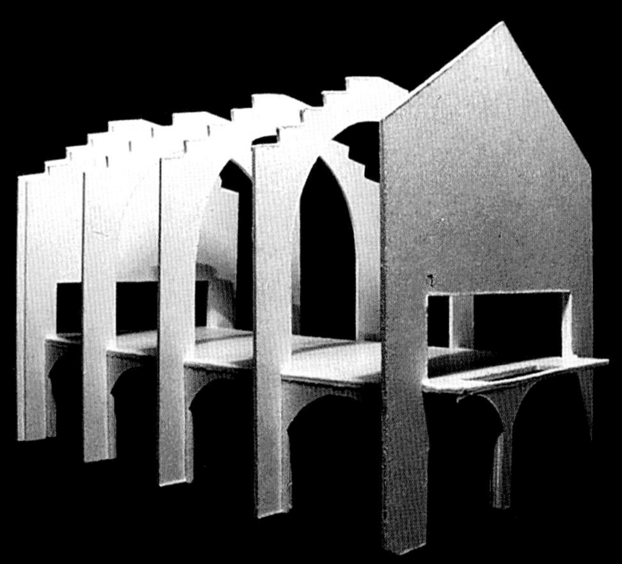

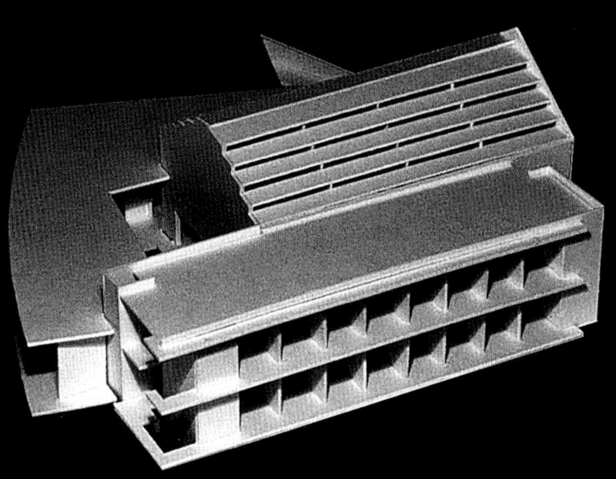

## Prototype School in Lloret
## Generalitat de Catalunya 1990

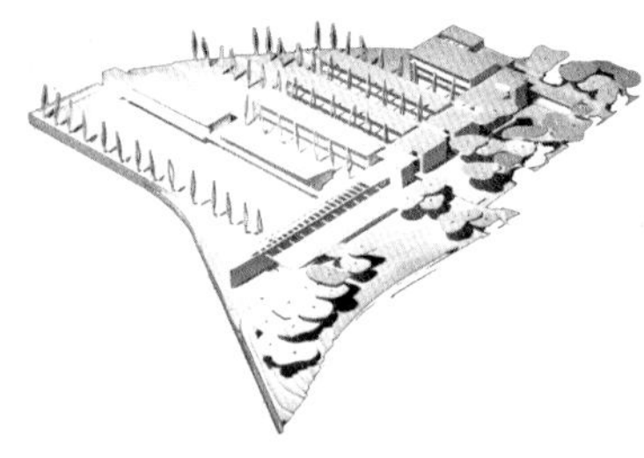

In a town on the Costa Brava and on a sloping plot of land populated with pine trees, the construction of a prototype school for the new Education Law was proposed. A set of buildings are organized in staggered strips on the slope, generating linear patios whose background will be the forest mass.

A set of ramps sews the different pavilions for classrooms, workshops, laboratories, gym, library, etc.

The project aims to obtain a fluid and global relationship between the interior and exterior spaces, the whole forming a small campus in which the different uses follow one another in a natural way.

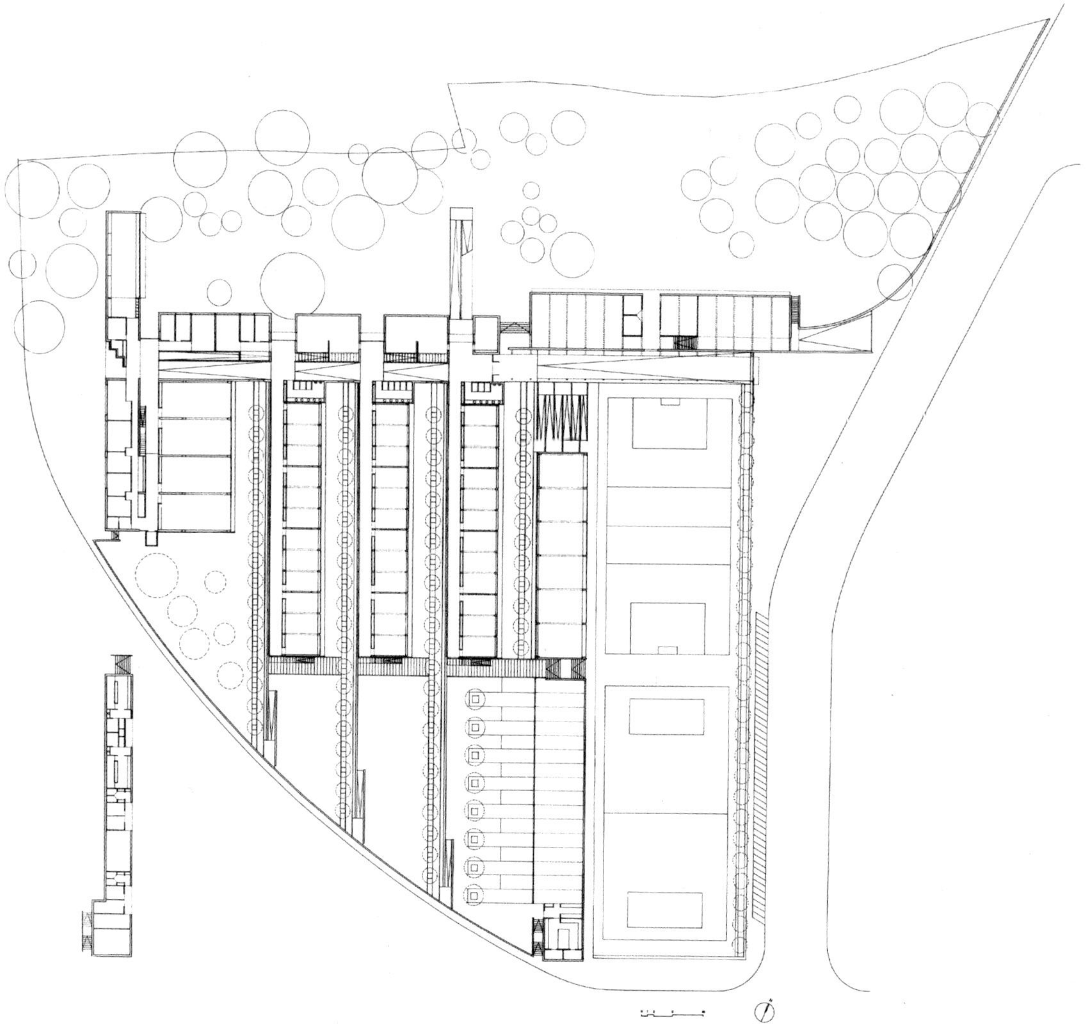

Schoolyard level

Ground floor

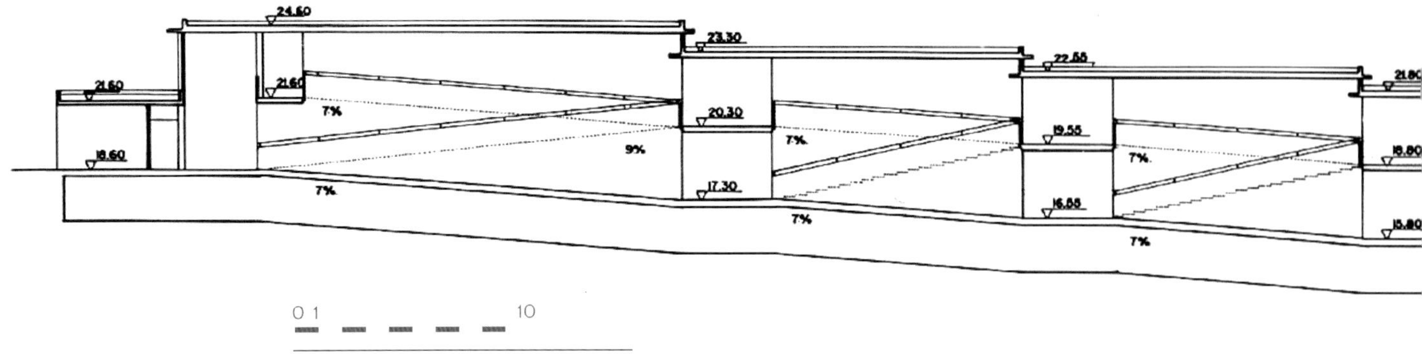


Promenade longitudinal section

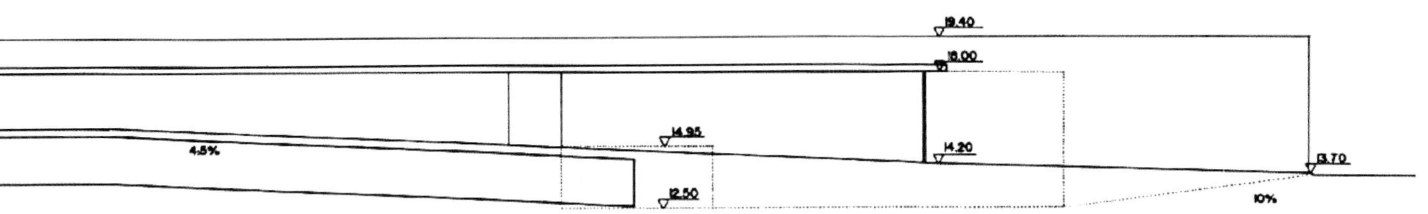
19.40
18.00
14.95
4.5%
14.20
13.70
12.50
10%

# Bertran Street Barcelona

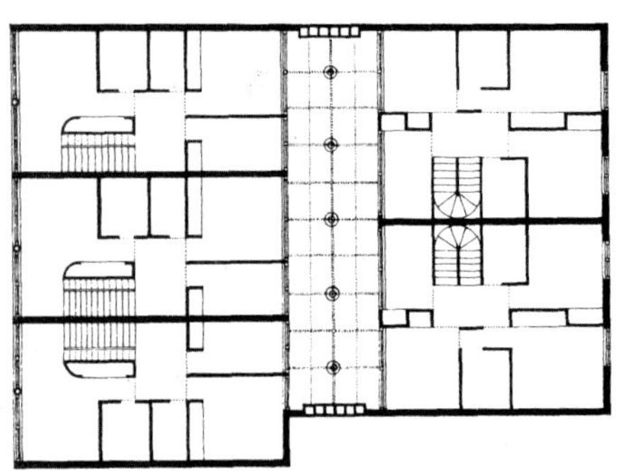

Second floor

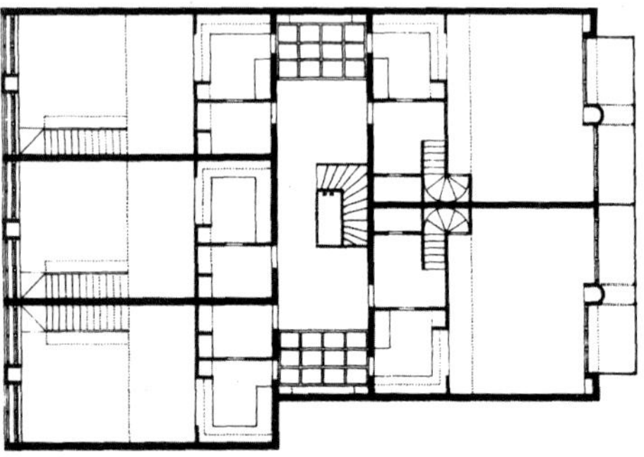

First floor

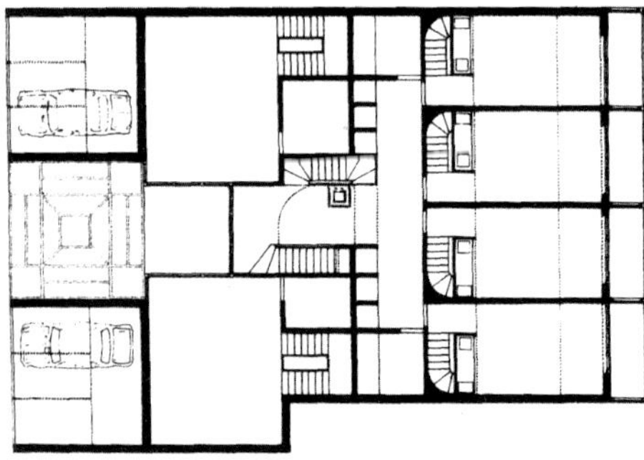

Ground floor

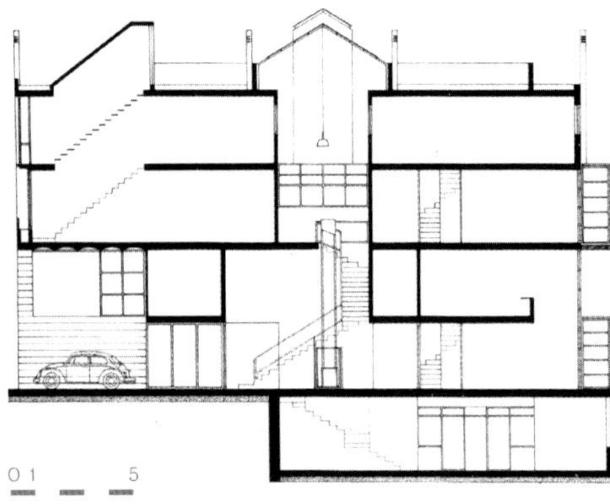

## Bertran 67–113
## 1981–1982 / 1983–1985

The project aims at the conjoining of aspects of the Mediterranean house-building tradition—like the entrance atrium, the inner street providing access to the dwellings, and the patio-cum-garden of the Roman house.

Listing some of the intentions of the project that prefigure the final result:

1 – Compliance with the regulation to do with parking spaces, avoiding the trauma of the ramp, and the utilization of a small inter-party-wall basement led me to the solution of the lateral garages on the ground floor.

2 – The entrance atrium enables us to sidestep the issue of the tiered mezzanine, thus improving the quality of the duplex premises as a small gallery.

3 – The routing of the general stairs and the replacement of the elevator by a small external freight elevator frees up the center, leading to a more comprehensive and clearer reading from the vestibule.

4 – The sum of the circulatory spaces and the obligatory patio areas leads to greater generosity in the handling of communal space, turning it into an interior courtyard street.

5 – The choice of a duplex typology for the dwellings, providing each of them with its proportional bit of flat roof-cum-sundeck, turns them into row houses, almost.

6 – The recouping of the garden-patio on the inside of the block, making use of the existing change of level, permits the siting of the basement premises and the small studios in duplex form with access from the ground floor.

The notions of the Modern Movement: the concrete framework, the duplex structure, the reclamation of the flat roof.

Similarly, the act of building is conceived of as an artisanal process with a preponderance of skills, utilizing old techniques like pressed lime stucco, facings, and marble gravel paving.

Plus more sophisticated techniques in the treatment of plastic, glass and aluminum.

113 Bertran Street

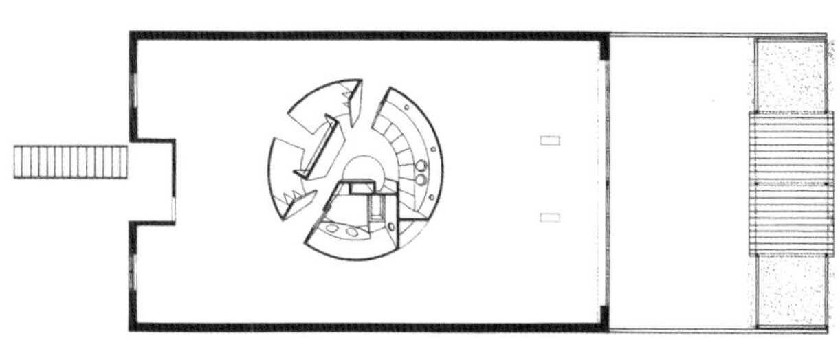

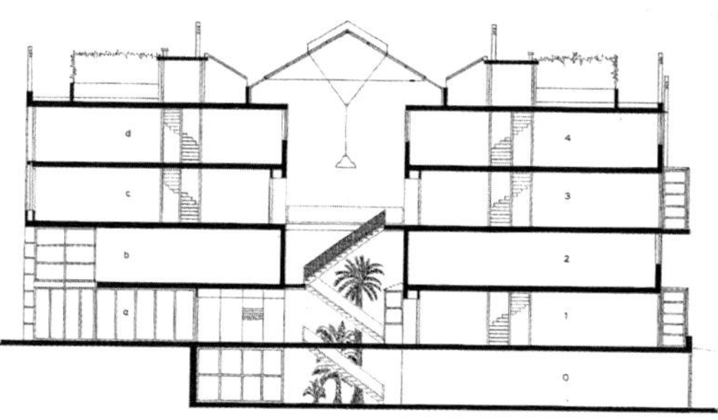

Camera House. José Manuel Ferrater, Photographer

Section

# Interiors 1992-1998

## Lola Restaurant Barcelona. 1992

This project strikes a balance between the building from the beginning of the 20th century and the construction of an aedicule, intended as a dining room, in the patio to the rear.

A denticulated, radial floor plan arranges the confines of the patio origami-style, with the front façade adopting a circular shape that recreates a small "piazzetta." Radial latticework beams knit the irregular perimeter together by adjusting their individual length, thus lending themselves to the construction of a polygonal, faceted roof.

This play of beams and shingles is conducive to different light effects, endowing the interior with a south lighting combined with the north light of the main façade, and the illumination that enters through the bamboo canes in the remaining façades.

The solution for the roof was to use modular lattice girders with small profiles. The faceted pieces of the roof were therefore housed between the upper chord and the lower brace of the fan trusses.

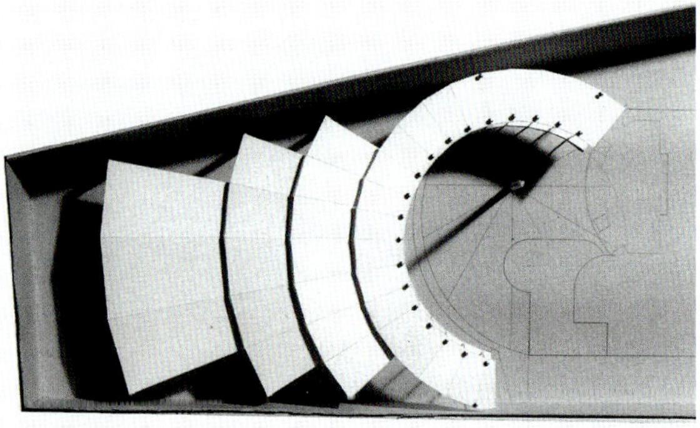

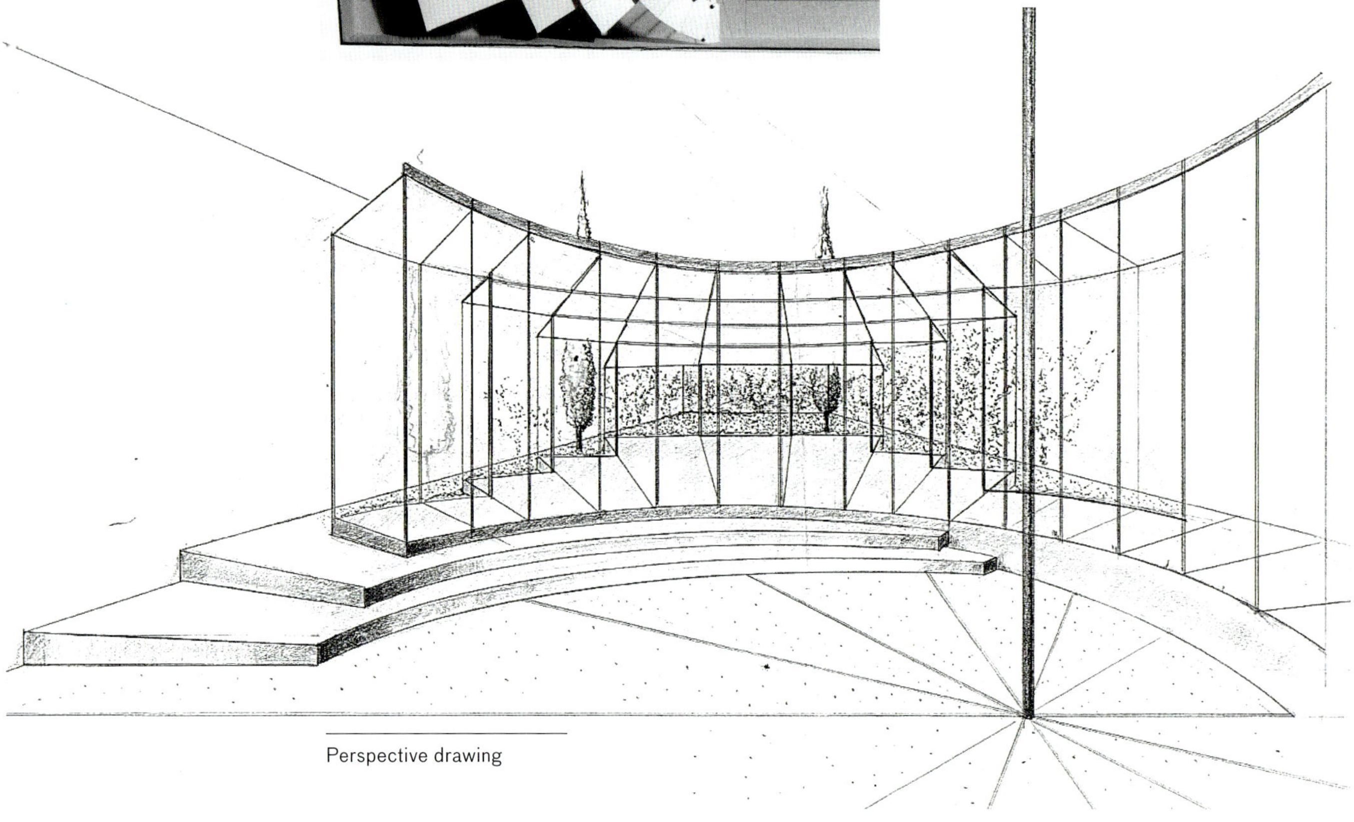

Perspective drawing

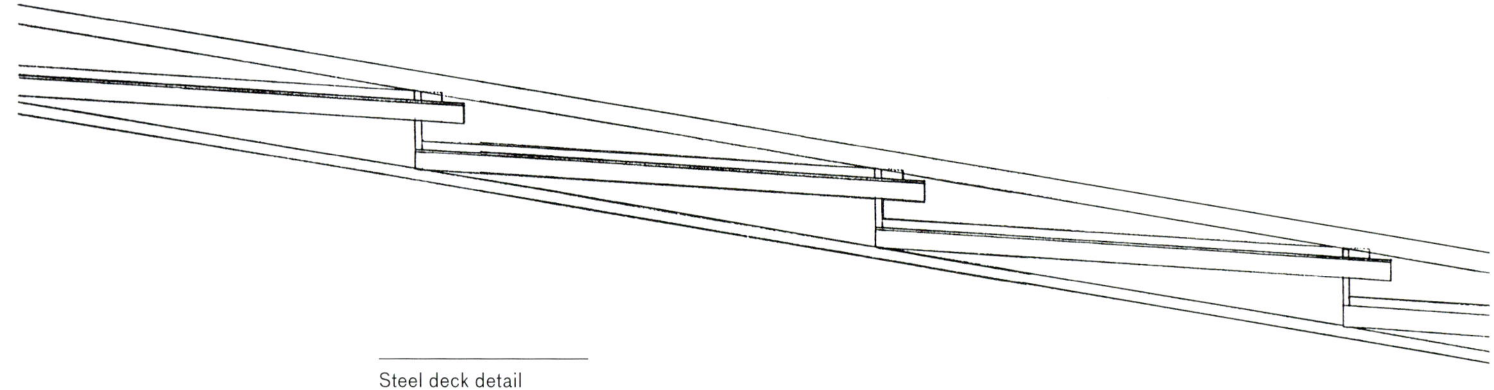

Steel deck detail

## Graphic Space
## Barcelona. 1993

The new graphical studio occupy first-floor premises in the lower part of Barcelona's Gracia district, previously used as a textile workshop.

The existing building is divided into two clearly differentiated areas. The first, corresponding to the access from the street, is long and narrow and has little natural light. This area provides access to the main space, consisting of a large unit with sides measuring 20 metres and almost five metres of clear height inside and a roof consisting of a series of parallel vaults, supported on a grid of laminated profiles resting on nine slender cast-iron columns.

This space receives natural lighting through skylights in the roof and an internal courtyard. The solution adopted consists of grouping all the main activities in the large interior building, leaving the access area for reception, services and small mobile meeting rooms, as well as a large longitudinal cupboard that runs along the entire space.

The large unit is equipped with furniture consisting of a series of fully mobile items made up of various cut and shaped laminar elements, developed around elevated volumes and supported by wheels. These elements, which include drawing tables with built-in screens, shelves, filing cabinets and cupboards, can create a work environment of their own, like a micro-space that accompanies the individual.

At the same time, they allow the use of space in a multitude of different combinations, adapting easily to any required change. The absolute mobility of these elements also makes it possible to freely modify the space where they relate to one another. That means the general atmosphere of the office environment can be entirely changed.

The architect Yago Conde (†) took part in this project in a substantive way.

Previous pencil hand sketches

# The Lawyers Association of Catalunya
Barcelona. 1998

The existing site is located en calle Roger de Llúria 106, near the Colegio de Abogados. It consists of a ground floor, a low-height partial basement level, and a small attic space with occupancy problems because of the presence of structural items (girders and beams). The site is 50 m. deep, narrow, with little exposure to the street, and lacking intermediate courtyards.

The project proposes an intervention limited in size, but radically changing the spatial perception of the existing site. The project also attempts to optimize the use of the different spaces, organizing the various activities into different zones within the building. The most radical intervention is located in the central area. It consists of a 9,5 x 3 m opening in the floor, which allows visual and spatial communication between the persons on the entrance level and those in the area of medical consultation on the lower level. A small excavation allows the floor to ceiling height required by code (2,5 m) to be achieved. This spatial void creates a visual connection between the archive in the attic and the break area, connected by a suspended walkway.

This intervention creates a triple height space that gathers the circulation elements: the stair-ramp, corridors, stairs, and walkways, all of which allow visual communication between the areas of client services, work areas, the conference area, and the archive. Finally, in the rear of the project, the administrative department and the main meeting room are located. They face the interior of the block and are illuminated by large skylights. At the back of the site, the administrative departments open into a courtyard in order to optimise their lighting and comfort conditions.

Inés Arquer

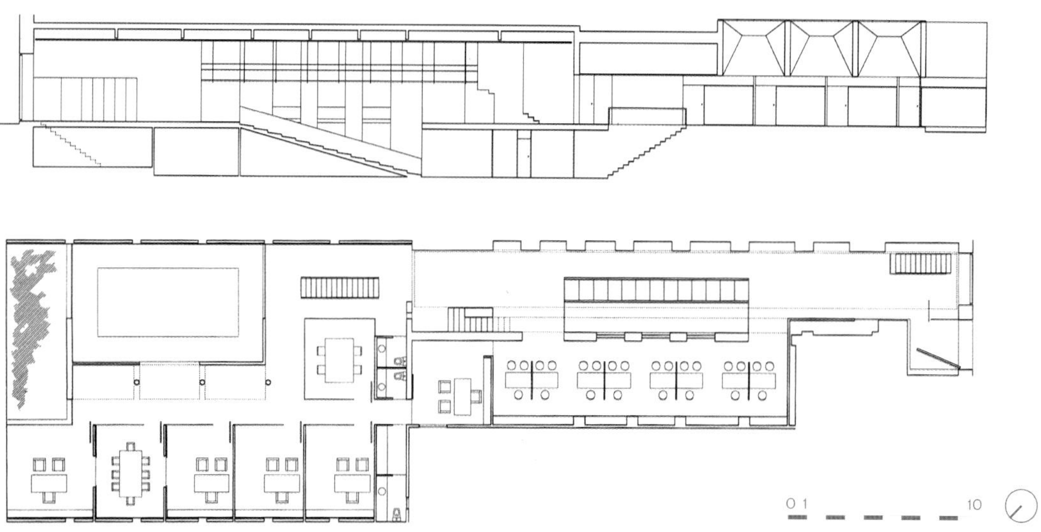


Section and ground floor

MÚTUA DE PREVISIÓ SOCIAL DELS ADVOCATS DE CATALUNYA

# Single Family Houses 1990-2000

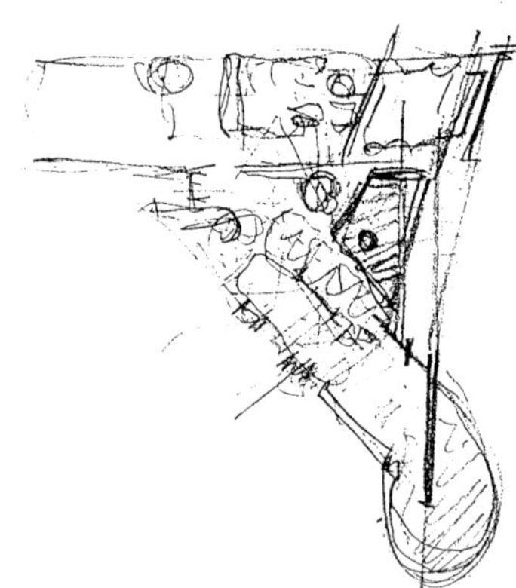

## Binisafua House Menorca. 1990

The house of aprox. 130 m2 is developed on a single level with a typical program for a second residence. It is located on the southern coast of Minorca, between Cap d'en Font and Binisafua's beach, lying over the rocky coast of a small bay flanked by islets.

The building rests on a Mars stone base built over the rocks. This absorbs the irregularities and slight changes in level of the site.

This continuous perimetral base becomes an intermediate space which provides entries and pergolas. From the outside it's the sheer simplicity and proportions of its white walls which contribute to a good integration of the building with the landscape.

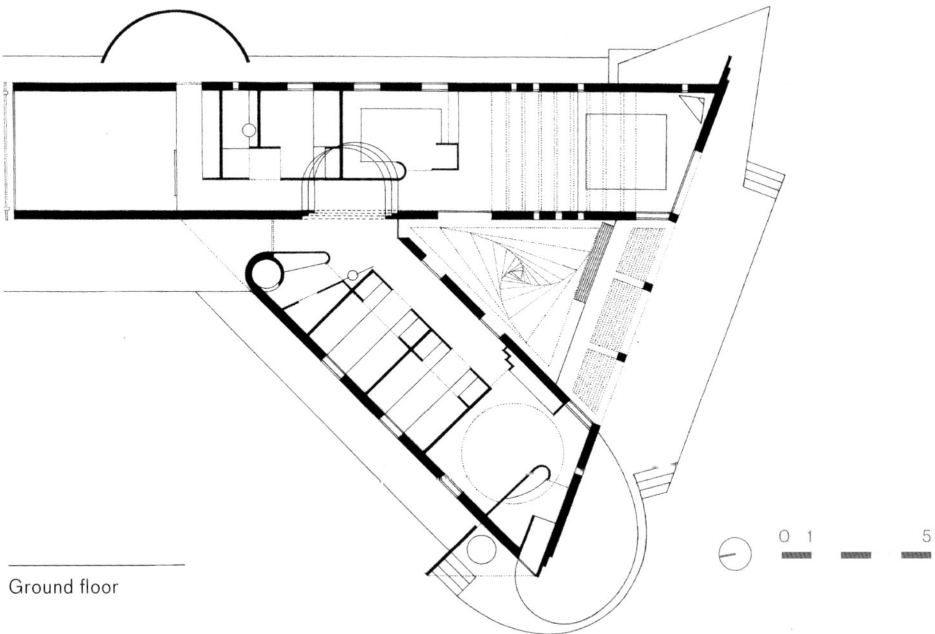


Ground floor

## Alonso-Planas House Barcelona. 1996

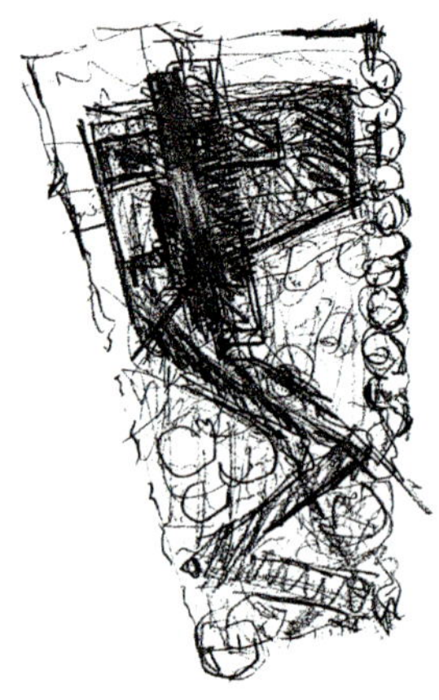

The deep trapezoid shaped site has a 16 meter drop in level between the lower access an the highest point of a ridge on a hill near Barcelona. From the highest point there are views of the two valleys, with vistas over the city and the Llobregat.

The main body of the house is located at the top of the site, literally fixed perpendicular to the slope. Because of this, the zig-zag access from the lower levels becomes very relevant.

This path flanked by holm oaks will form a small wood which will hide the nearby views to the buildings in the gulley, allowing an improved orientation ant the long vistas. The path ends entering the underground floor levels.

The largest part, the paint and sculpture workshop, is located following the topography and protruding slightly from the site. It is lit by a large horizontal opening. The outdoor areas and swimming pool are organised over the workshop.

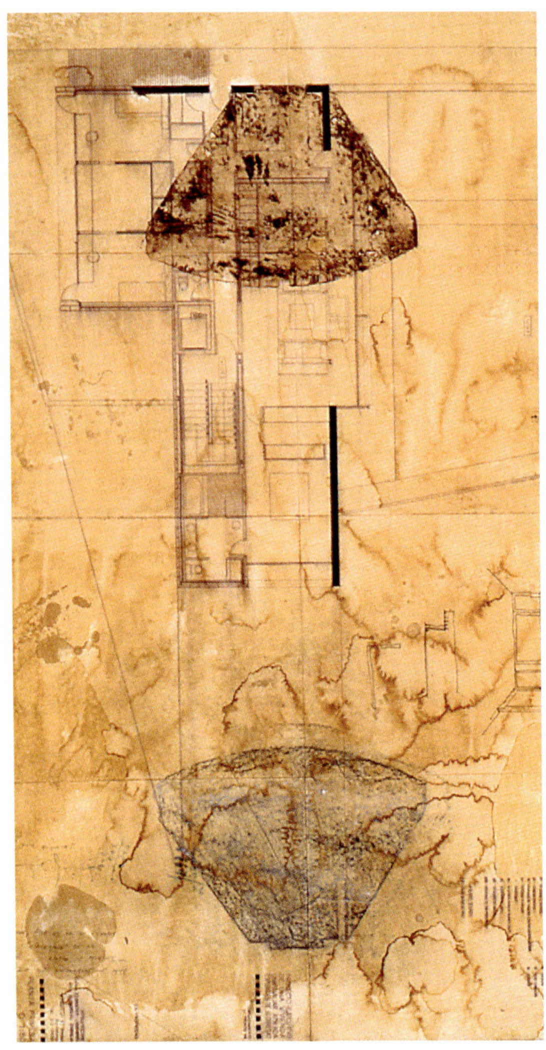

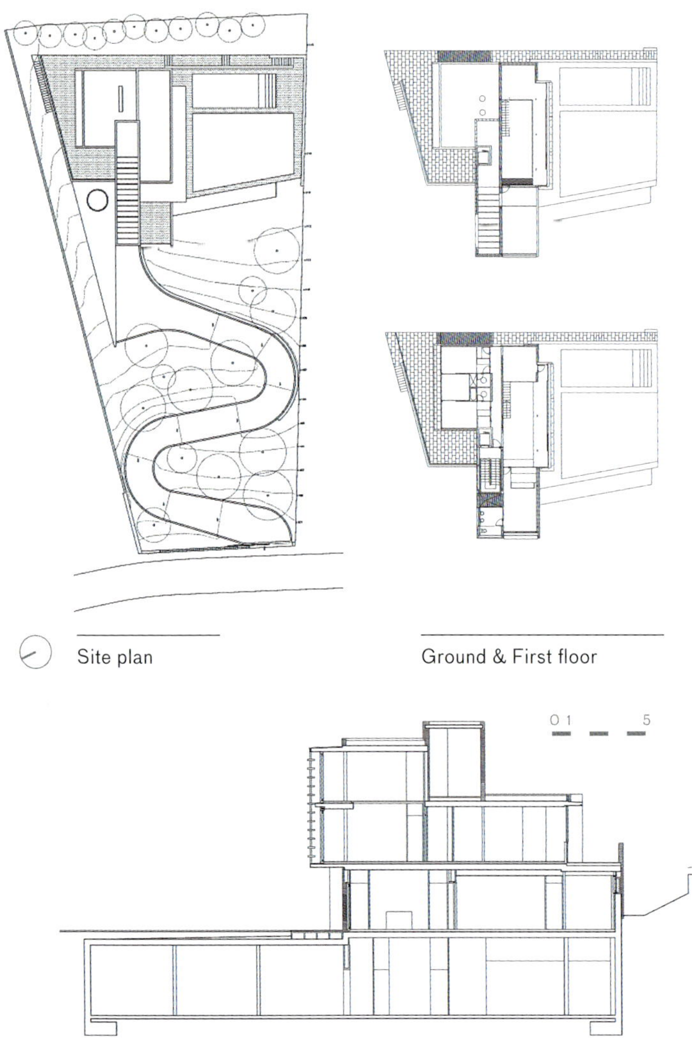

## Tagomago House Ibiza 1999

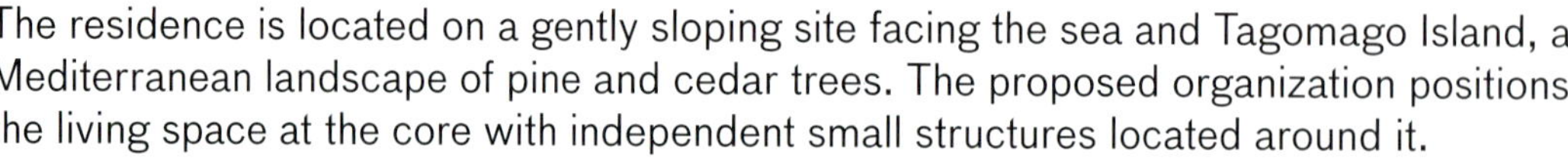

The residence is located on a gently sloping site facing the sea and Tagomago Island, a Mediterranean landscape of pine and cedar trees. The proposed organization positions the living space at the core with independent small structures located around it.

Given that the house is intended to be a vacation residence this allows for more flexible use, depending upon the number of occupants. The articulation of the house along a longitudinal axis provides ideally individual units independent from the core.

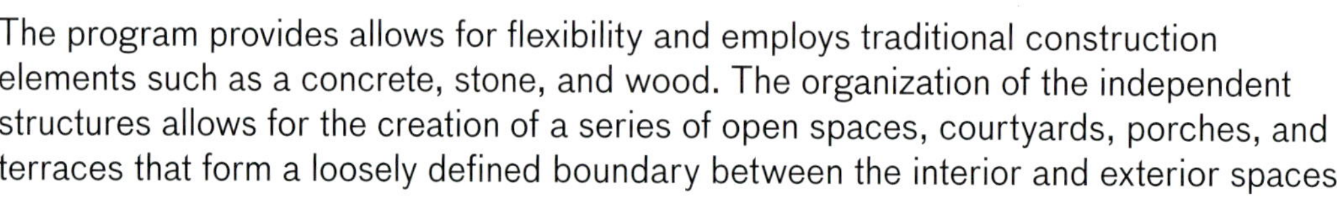

The program provides allows for flexibility and employs traditional construction elements such as a concrete, stone, and wood. The organization of the independent structures allows for the creation of a series of open spaces, courtyards, porches, and terraces that form a loosely defined boundary between the interior and exterior spaces.

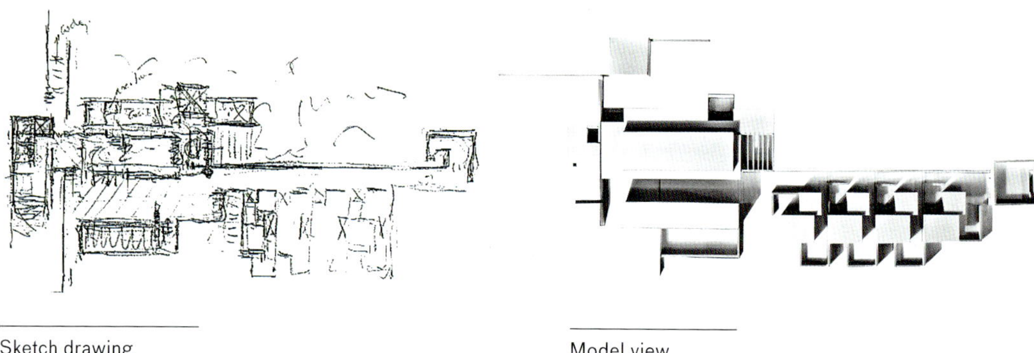

Sketch drawing

Model view

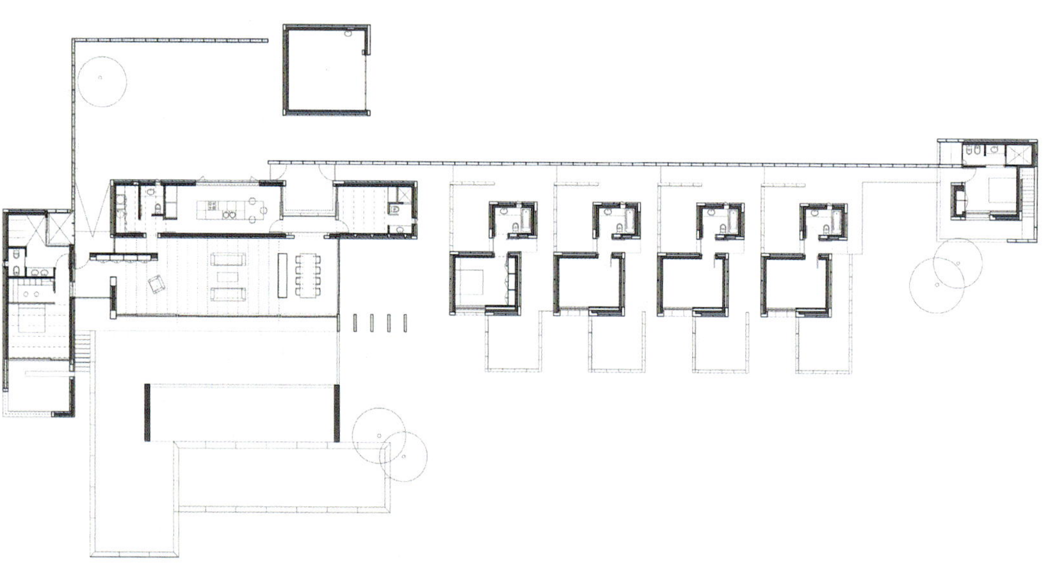

Ground floor

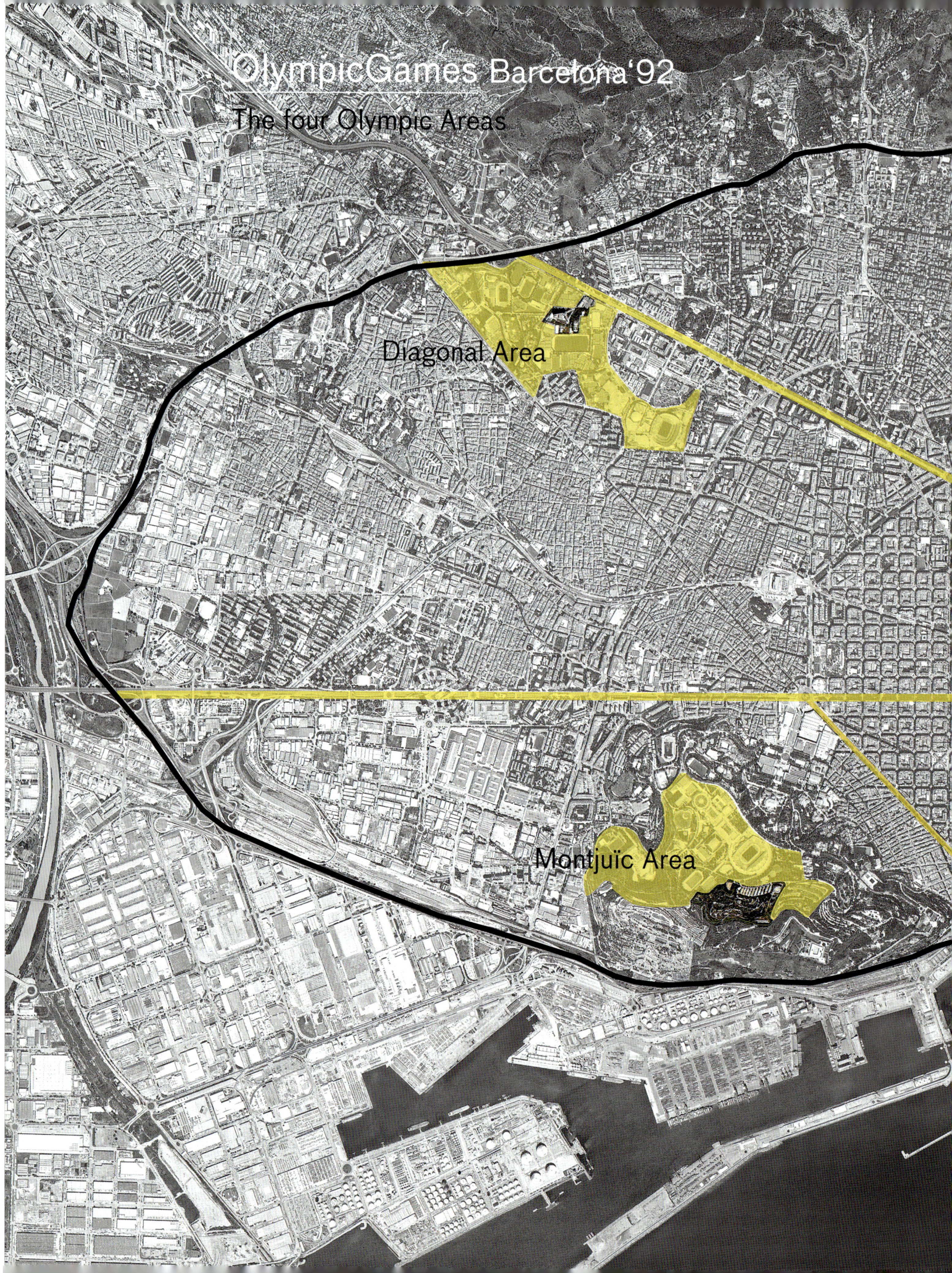
OlympicGames Barcelona'92
The four Olympic Areas
Diagonal Area
Montjuïc Area

Vall d'Hebrón Area
Poblenou Area
Montjuïc Area
Olympic Cross (1992)
into Botanical Garden of Barcelona
14Ha
Diagonal Area
Olympic Hotel & Fontserè Gardens (1992)
into Hotel & Catalunya Convention Center
450 Keys
Vall d'Hebrón Area
Journalists Olympic Village (1992)
into Residences & Public Space
489 Units
Poblenou Area
Referees Olympic Village (1992)
into Residences & Torras Gardens
560 Units

## Vall d'Hebrón Olympic Area
## Journalists Olympic Village (1992) into Residences & Public Space

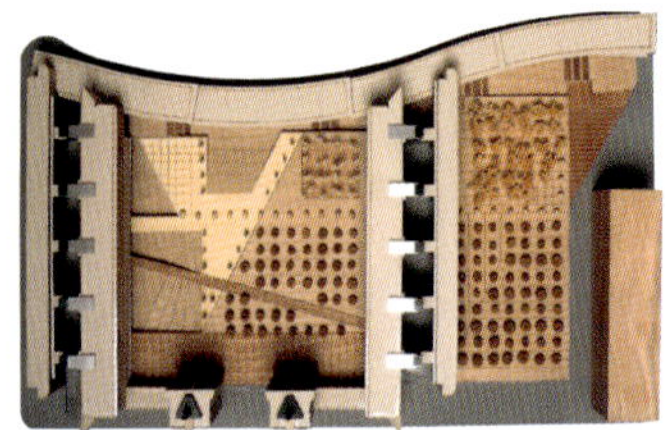

In this area on the outskirts of Barcelona there was a settlement of blocks from the 1970s, without identity of any kind, without facilities, or public space.

The journalists' residential villa project for the games tries to achieve these attributes.

The project is located in an area of great changes, responding to the diverse demands of its context.

A large sinuous building, with a marked linearity, adapts to the slope and closes the complex on the northern side.

Two groups of double slabs, of different section and bay size, close the sides of the square. These slabs have their vertical circulation cores in the central patios.

A small, linear slab, connects the different buildings, closing the square and acting as base and support of the two isolated towers.

After the Olympic Games the 20% of the residences was destinated to Social Housing.

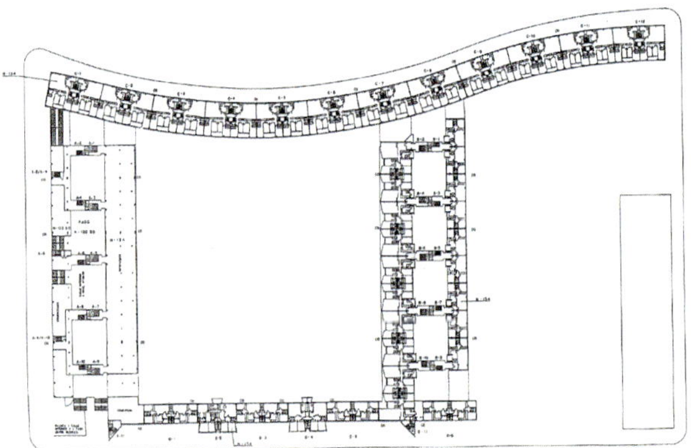

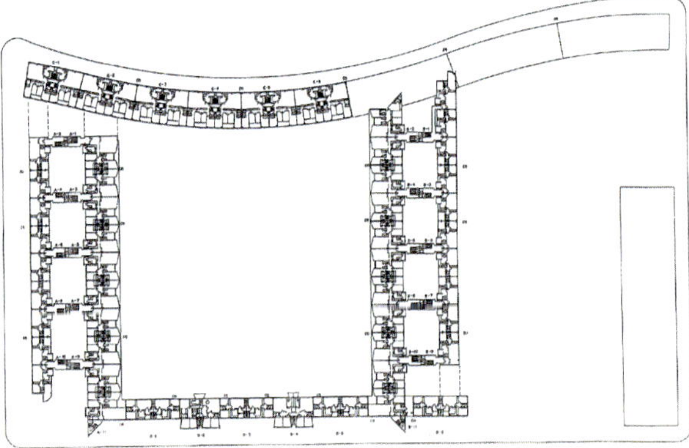

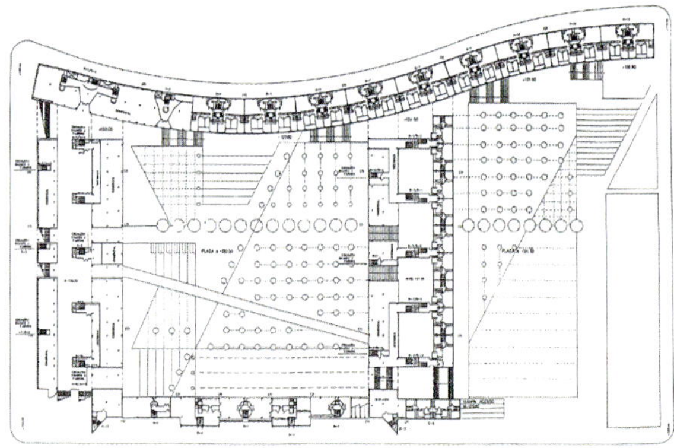

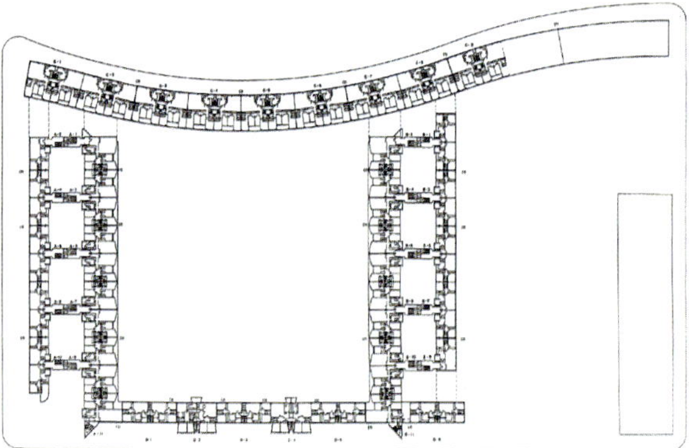

Floor plans

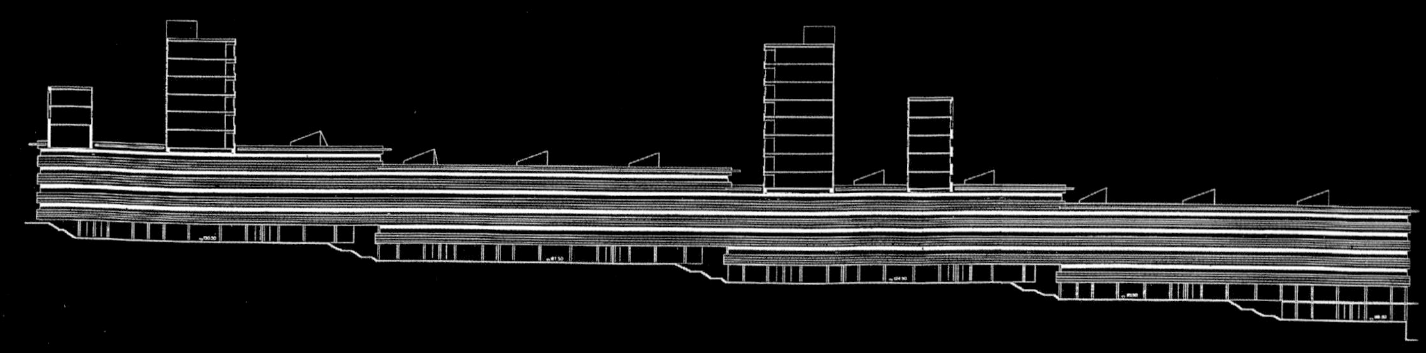

Block C. Interior Elevation

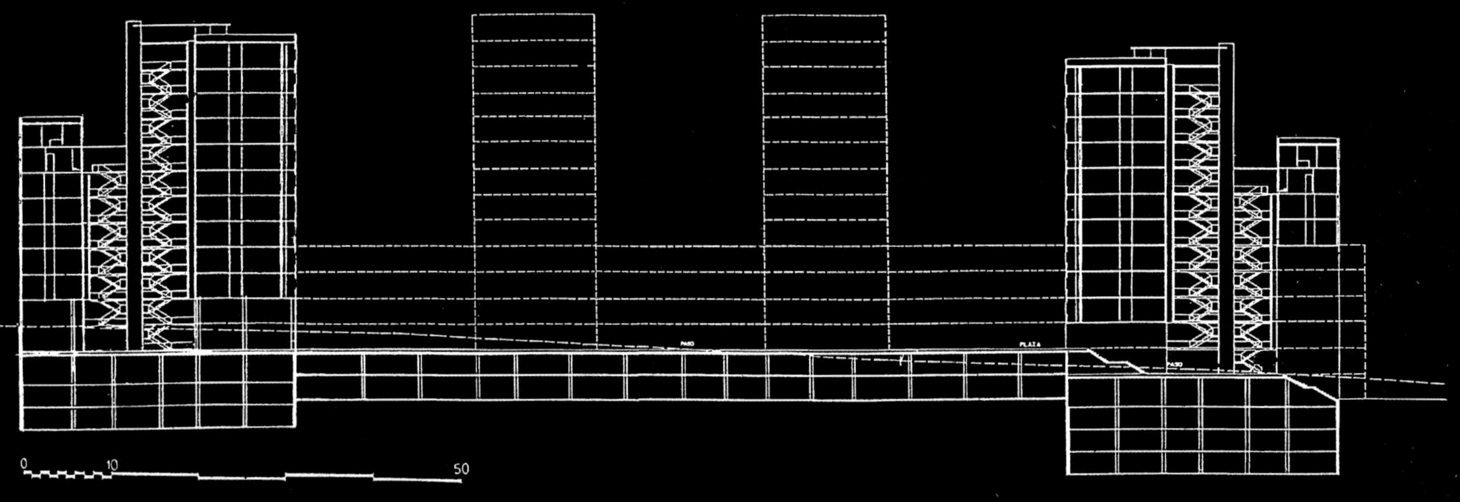


Cross Section

30 years later

## Diagonal Olympic Area
## Olympic Hotel & Fontserè Gardens (1992) into Hotel & Catalunya Convention Center

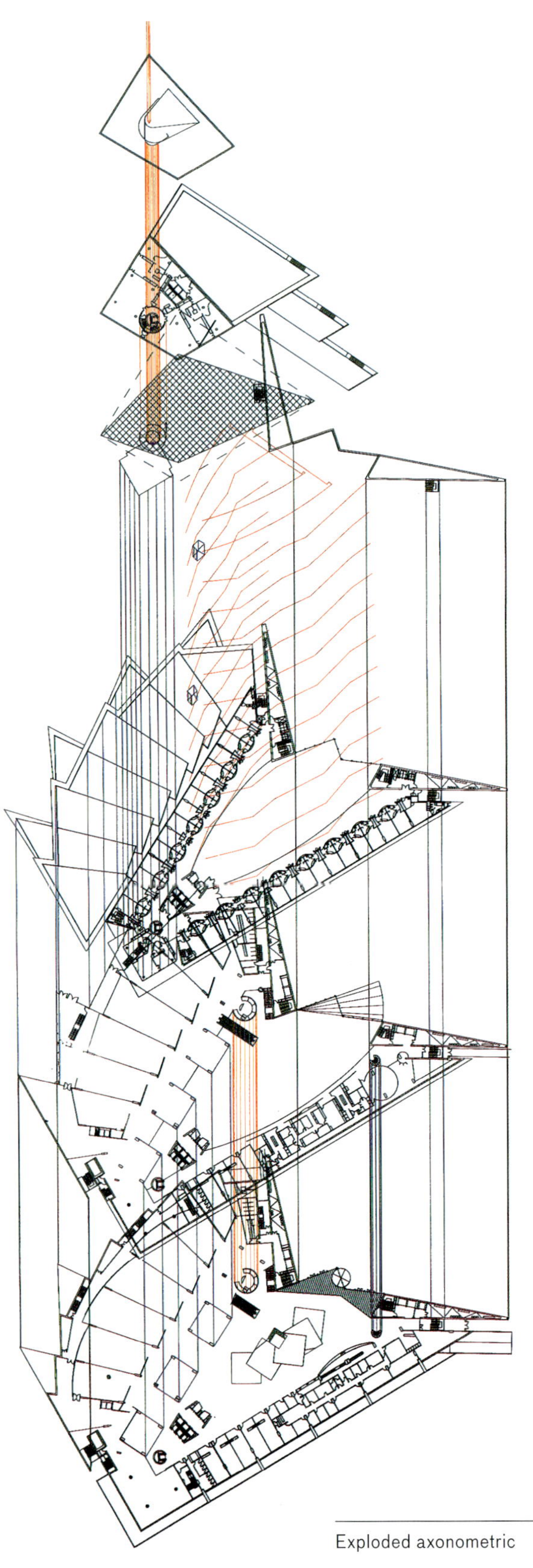

Exploded axonometric

The construction of the internal space is the result of a series of conceptual and constructive manoeuvres: the first one consists in sliding the shutterings of the room floor slabs in a game of polygonals which facet and align the different surfaces, forming the first internal facade. This group of changing planes confers a dynamic quality and contributes to control the acoustics of the large hall.

The second maneuver carried out is in relation to the section. The space is structures vertically into three parts by an inclined curved surface.

Lighting is obtained through the north facing curtain wall which acquires rigidity thanks to two folds. Wind loads are absorbed by horizontal nerves.

During daytime the space flows to the outside emphasizing the natural light, the facets, the edges and planes. At night the process is reversed, the space closes in on itself and the artificial lighting outlines and follow the lines.

There are two large concrete walls that allow the interrelation between users and service layouts. These walls form the main access facade on the outside producing a strong change of scale which contributes to locate the building on the site.

HOTEL REI JUAN CARLOS I

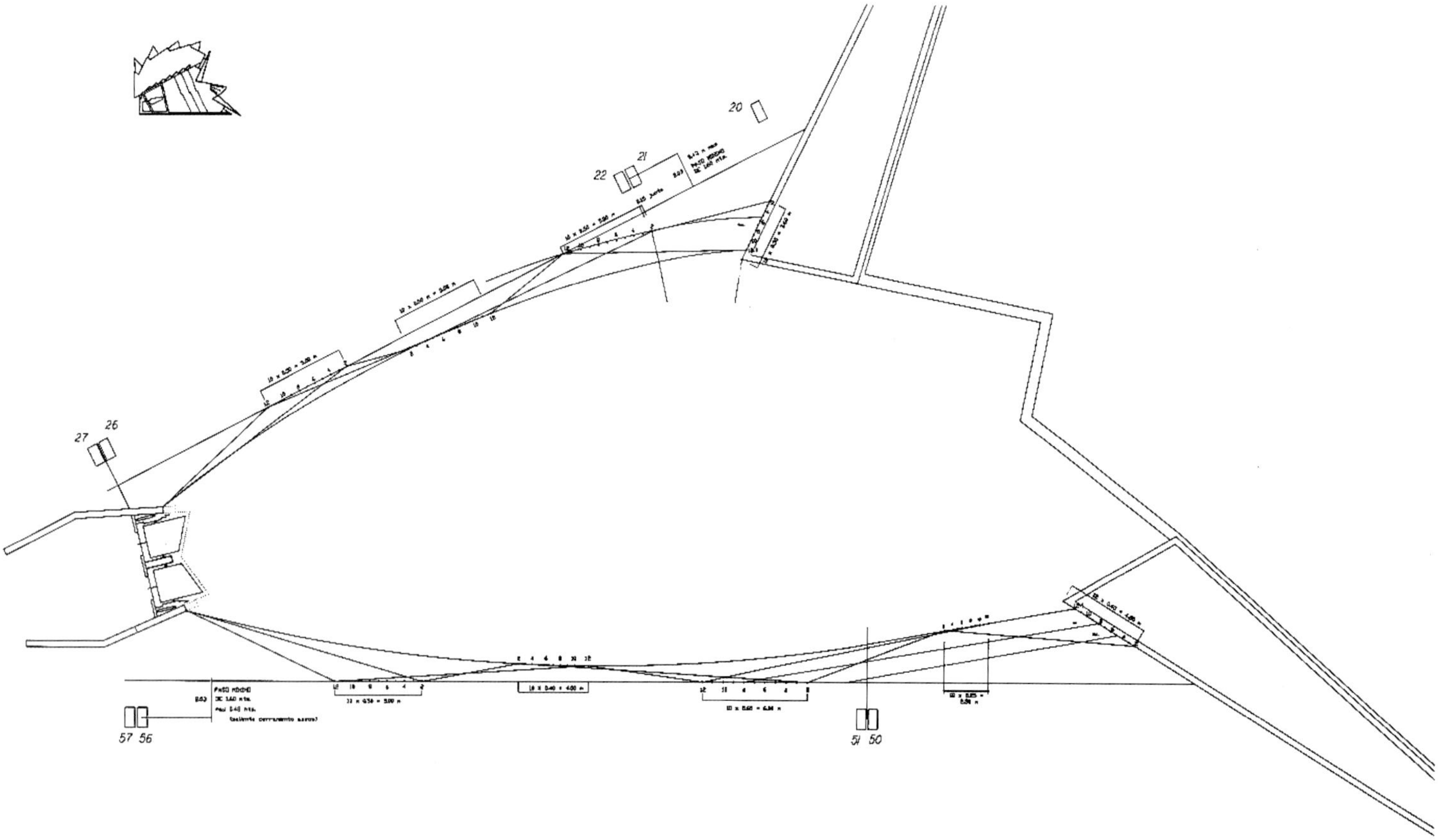

A five-star Hotel for 450 rooms was planned as part of a complex of gardens and other amenities in the Diagonal Avenue in Barcelona.

The building is composed of two wings which contain the guest accommodation, articulated by a14 storey glass tower in which the suites are located.

Between them, the two wings form the large central space, made up of polygonal which slide along two parabola arcs over the main floor.

A series of overlapping polygonal roofs rise up towards the south allowing natural light to enter from above.

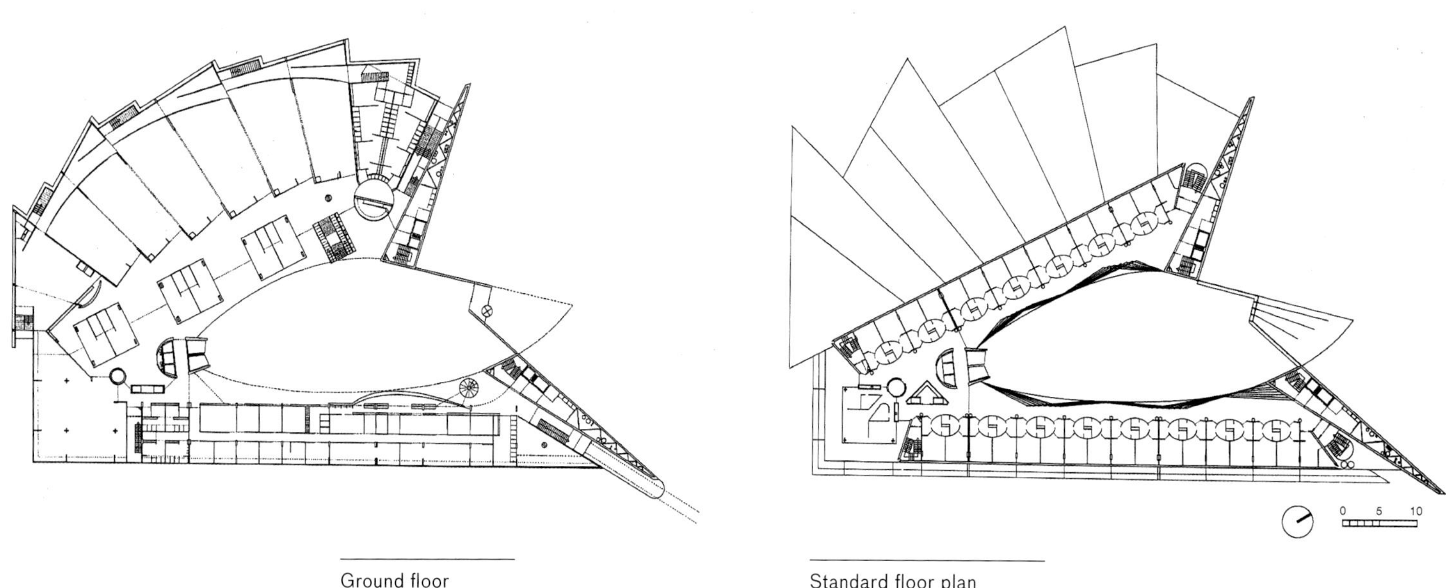


Ground floor

Standard floor plan

Path network. Topographic manipulation. First plantations

Sequoia . California

Reference to OAB book, "Revisinting the Barcelona Botanical Garden" from 1989 to 2019

## Poblenou Olympic Area
## Referees Olympic Village (1992) into Residences & Torras Gardens

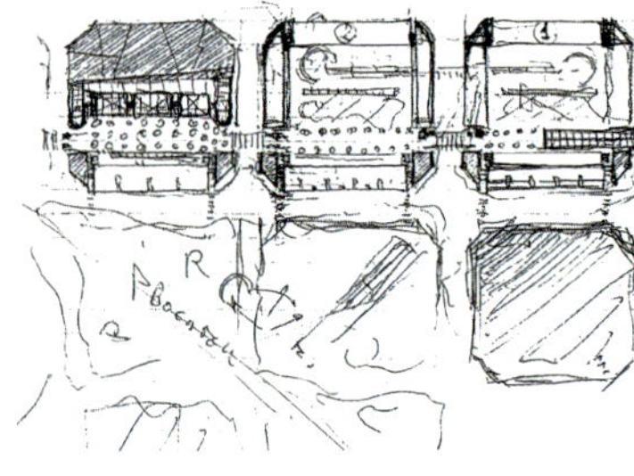

The residential project on an area of almost three blocks of Poble Nou, with 560 housing units of various types and large amounts of green spaces, is located on the site of the old Torras factory which manufactured steel structures.

From the moment of the project's conception we took into account that it could become a guideline for future interventions in an area for ambiguous character: an old industrial area, adjoining the Villa Olimpica, which transforms itself into a residential area. For this reason, taking as compulsory reference the Special Urban Ordering Plan of the Maritime façade of Barcelona, various novelties were introduced with the intention of reinterpreting the essential aspects of the Cerda block.

Firstly we thought out rigorously flat types of two, three and four bedrooms, duplex and studios, located in 12,6 m. deep linear blocks. This depth permits a rational distribution without ventilation patios and with all the main spaces opening to a façade.

In the morphological proposal we introduced a transcendental novelty: to break the continuity of the sea-oriented elevations by introducing passages which define slender towers at the corners. This introduces a singular rhythmic element which emphasises the chamfer, the essential element of the Cerda block, creating another pedestrian itinerary precisely at the zebra crossings.

Because of all this, the general form of the complex appears as the final result in which the diverse problems are resolved: constructive-5 m. structural grid, functional- variety of typologies, correct functioning of the car parking... Aesthetic- searching an attractive volumetric solution. In the façades we have attempted to make predominant the compositional order of large openings in the lower floors and small openings in the crowning part of the duplex.

For the construction of this large complex, emphasised by its unity and formal presence, we devised large prefabricated elements to resolve both internal and external façades. The free space remaining has also been carefully designed, considering it as an autonomous architectural project.

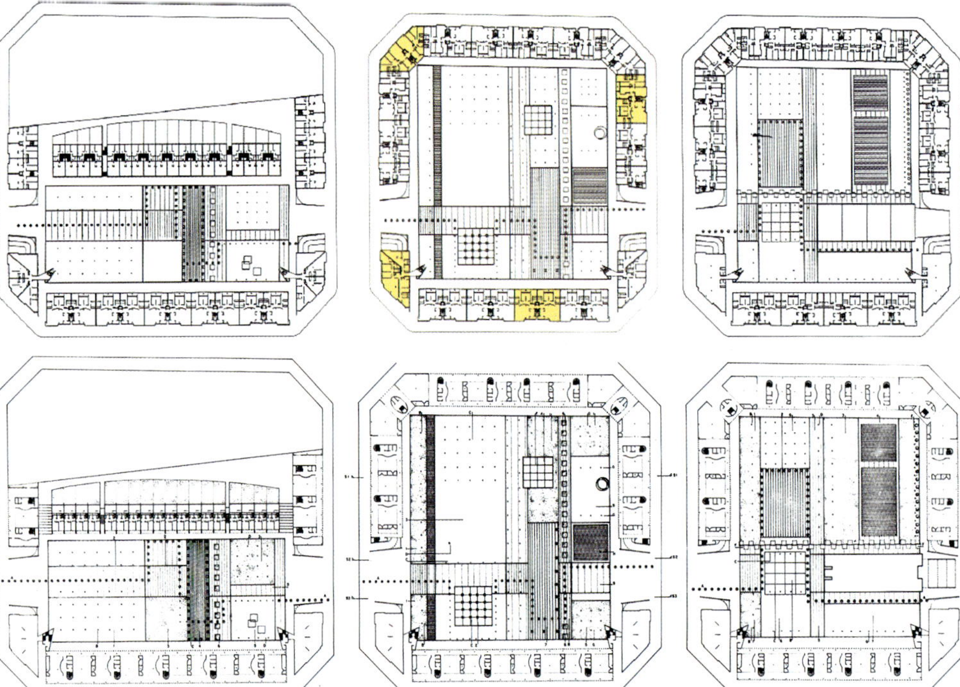

Blocks. Standard floor

0 5 — — — — — 50

Blocks. Ground floor

Original sketches of the gardens

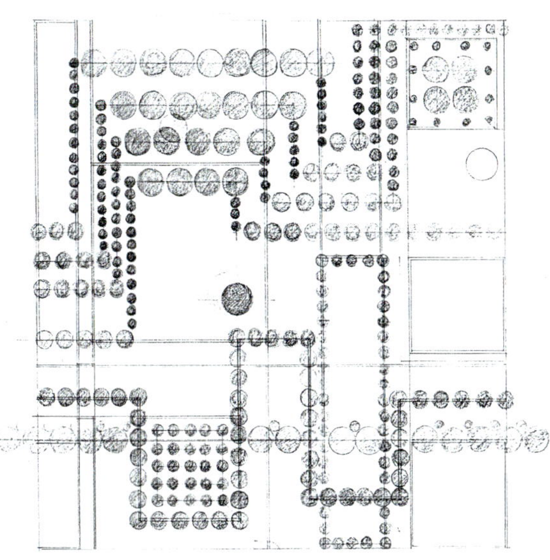

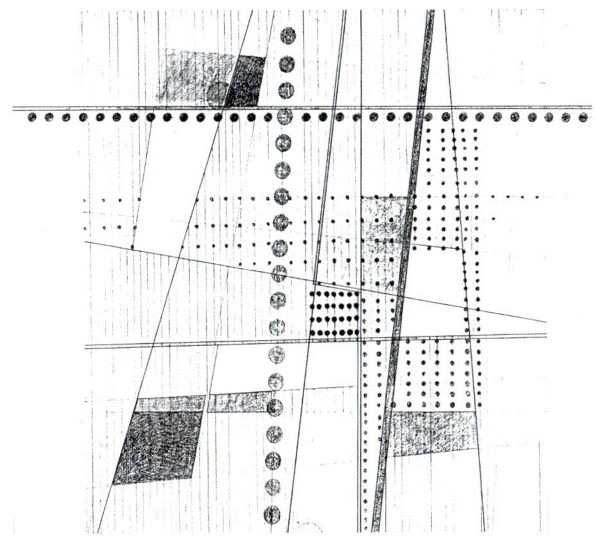

# Banyoles Olympic Village

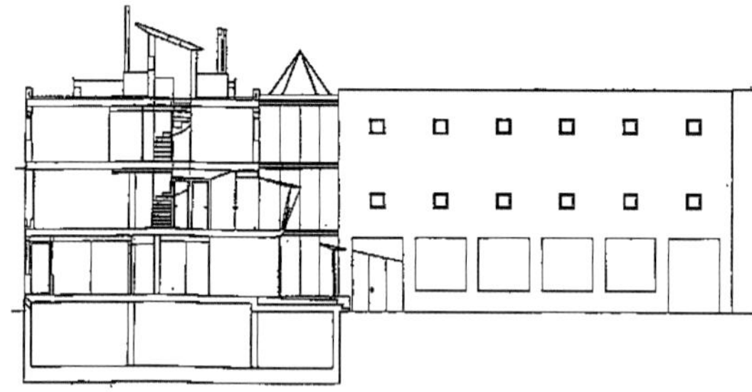

Floor plan

The Selection Committee, who invited us to participate in the creation of the Olympic Village at Banyoles, awarded us «Island 7», a remnant left as result of various urban interventions.
The demolition of the existing factory sheds, combined with the new street layout, produced an L-shaped site.

The new building then had to establish a connection with the party walls inside the block and at either end of the L.

The dimensions of the short side created a long narrow building which we used to fullfil the requirements of the housing brief as well as providing various points of access.

The project exploits a solution based on the theatricality of architecture to produce suitable solutions for specific problems, using the collection of mishaps to generate a new scenario, different to the one originally conceived.

One party wall is punctuated with a series of false windows to be opened when the interior is liberated. A series of colored planes slide over the old party walls forming a new silhouette along a passage which culminates with a single evergreen oak.

All the staircases make use of zenithal light to enhance the spaces: the main access has a large pyramidal skylight while the second access has six small skylights marking the route. The third staircase has a glazed opening at the front of its small prismatic roof.

The long corridor on the first floor presents itself as the centre of gravity of the project. It acts as an «in between» element, linking the upper and lower parts of the building, acting as a viewing balcony for the new urban scene.

As a counterpoint to the interior space, the street façades rhythmic orders of openings contribute to produce a sober, urban effect.

A «joinery» process unfolds as intermediate world of details, where the use of materials (steel, aluminum, wood, travertine, and rendered walls), in combinations, define the plastic dialogue of the building.

# New experimentations
# Manifests 1993-1996

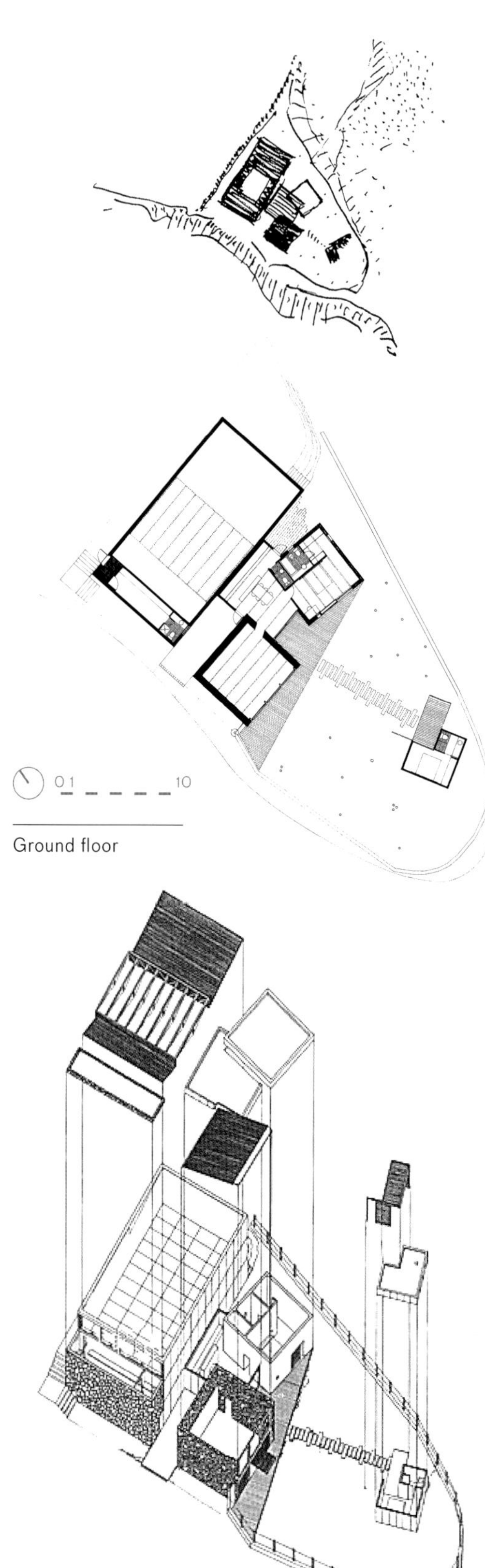


Ground floor

Exploded axonometric

## House-Studio in Llampaies. 1993

For some time I helped my brother José Manuel, a fashion photographer, to look for a site in which to build his residence and workplace. We finally found it in Llampaies, a village of the alto Ampurdà region. It consisted of a threshing circle shaped enclosure containing a derelict square hayloft built of stone facing the sun at noon.

The first decision was to keep and rebuild the old construction, and to elaborate the project from the fragmentation, in a way similar to vernacular architecture. The old building, almost five meters high, would receive a new-pitched roof hidden within its walls, becoming the living room of the house. Next to it, and slightly rotated, a new cubic volume houses the night areas. A lower volume which connects the other two houses the entries, acting as hallway and dinner, with the kitchen at the back. The large blind box used as photographic studio emerges at the back of the site, taking advantage of a three-meter drop in level to shelter the cluster. This space is structured from its roof section, allowing an almost central position of the light catchment area as well as maximum height and depth of field at the back of the grey finished studio. At the opposite end a clerestory window facing West will flood the studio with warm sunset light. A series of cable driven shades will provide control of the natural daylight.

A small wooden volume used as guesthouse rises at the southern end of the patio garden, in front of the other buildings. It receives light through a sliding window overlooking the veranda and a small "crack" in the roof over the bathroom.

Finally, the meaning of the architectural intervention lies in the external treatment; the old fence around the site gets covered with ivy and two small groups of trees, seven facing east and sevenfacing west, contribute to provide a sense of magic like the one seen in the old photograph of this place which was often used as setting for the town holiday.

The materials used, fiber/cement panels, concrete beams, steel sections, lime based renders, brickwork, block work, wooden panels, or in situ concrete floors, will retain their original texture.

Some mobile elements such as sliding windows/doors, counterweighted sashes or louvers activated by compressed air pistons, will help to relate the interior to the exterior forming an intermediate space like a porch or terrace.

Image by José Manuel Ferrater

## Impiva Technological Park. 1994

The construction is proposed, for the Comunidad Valenciana of a prototype center which houses a group of new and technologically innovatory businesses of different kinds.

The project explores the relationship between interior and exterior space: the form, in short, of utilizing the building as a support for a heterogeneous program whose disinct elements – small, semi-industrial premises: laboratories; offices; institutional annexes and services – are interwoven in the built continuum of facades conceived as an abstract whole in which great emphasis is placed on the construction of the different membranes, converting the frontages as a whole into the formal expression of the building.

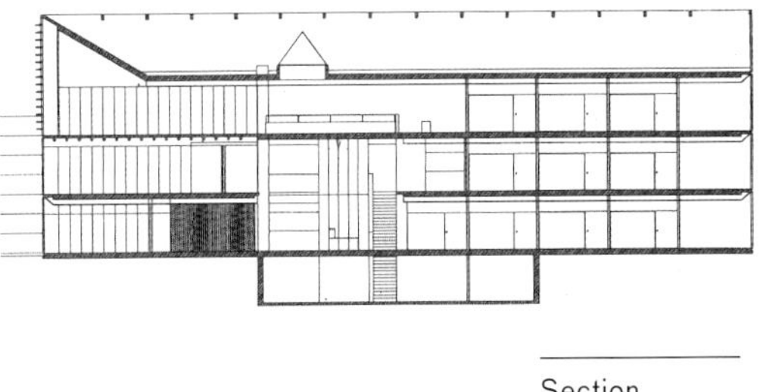

Section

Each frontage is reinforced inside by an extended repertoire of programs, and it is the interweaving of these that gives the feeling of space, the play of frontal and overhead light, the ambiguity of the setting in relation to the outside, and the relationship with the landscape.

Thus, the staggering of the different buildings acquires rotundity and force vis-à-vis their urban implantation in the intersection of the avenue leading to the Grao and the future Castellón bypass.

The asymmetrical geometry of the buildings generates a frontage which subsumes the main entrances and the park announcing them to the city, and a rear which organizes the secondary entrances, the parking lots and the unloading areas. Before they meet the buildings, both ground surfaces – lawn in front, and asphalt at the rear – are conceived as continuous carpets.

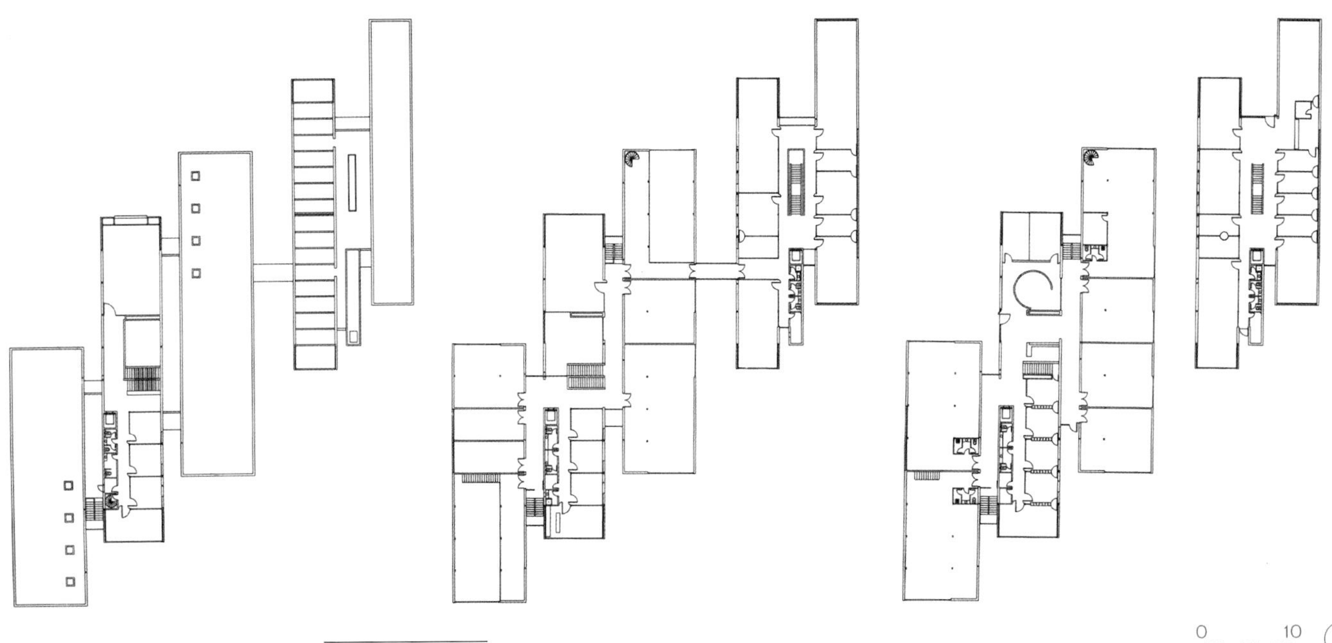


Floor plans

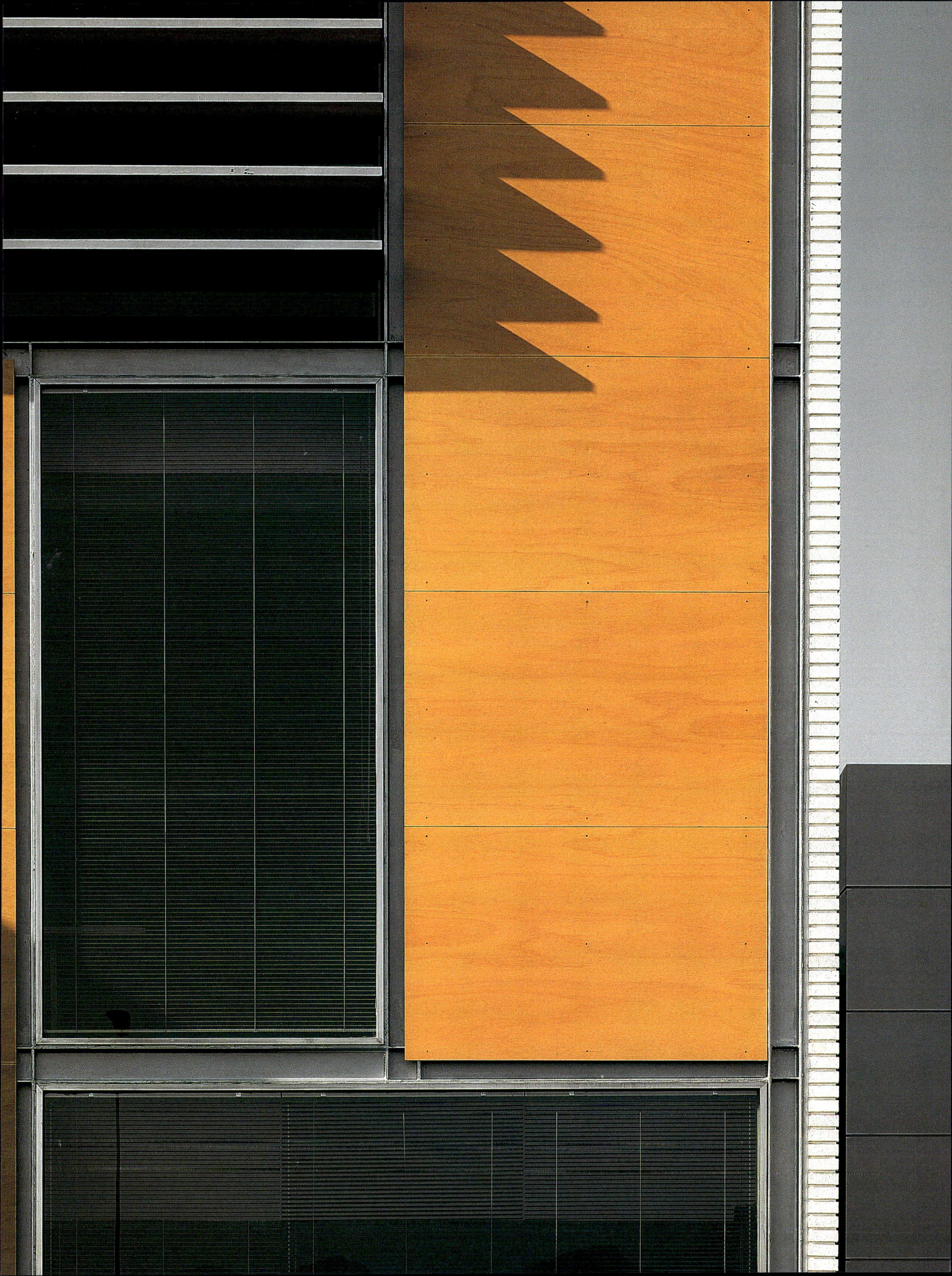

MODA INTIMA
C

## UAB Library Complex

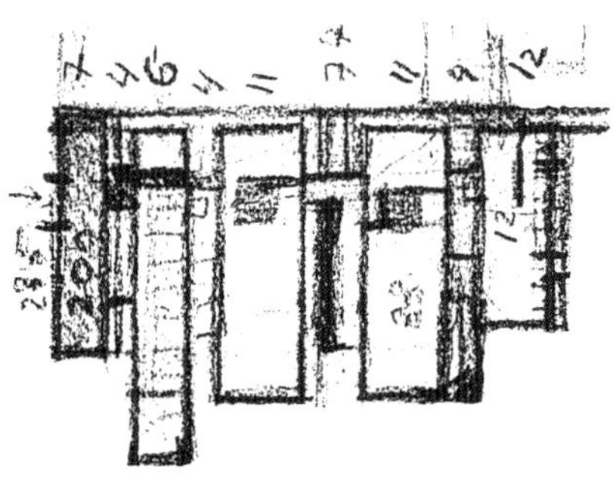

A library for the 21st century needs to be a complex of spaces that are flexible, capable of growth and transformation. A contemporary library cannot be a unified space, as in the designs of Boullée or Erik Gunnar Asplund's building in Stockholm.

As announced in Hans Scharoun's State Library in Berlin and subsequently developed in contemporary interventions, it has to involve the organization of widely differing spaces which thake a complex and diversified program into account and create spaces for all sorts of readers, from study rooms to specialized reading rooms for doctoral dessertations.

The project design organizes the complexity of the proposed program.

To achieve this, the most suitable spatial structure is of a sequence of five blocks, devoted to a study room and Documentation Center; a library; a newspaper an periodical archive; a book stack; management and adminstration services. Inside, articulating and binding this sequence together, open areas are created to forma a "street of libraries", an interior space which connects the five blocks and is bathed in natural light entering laterally from the courtyards and overhead from various skylights.

This street space serves as a huge linking and entrance hall.

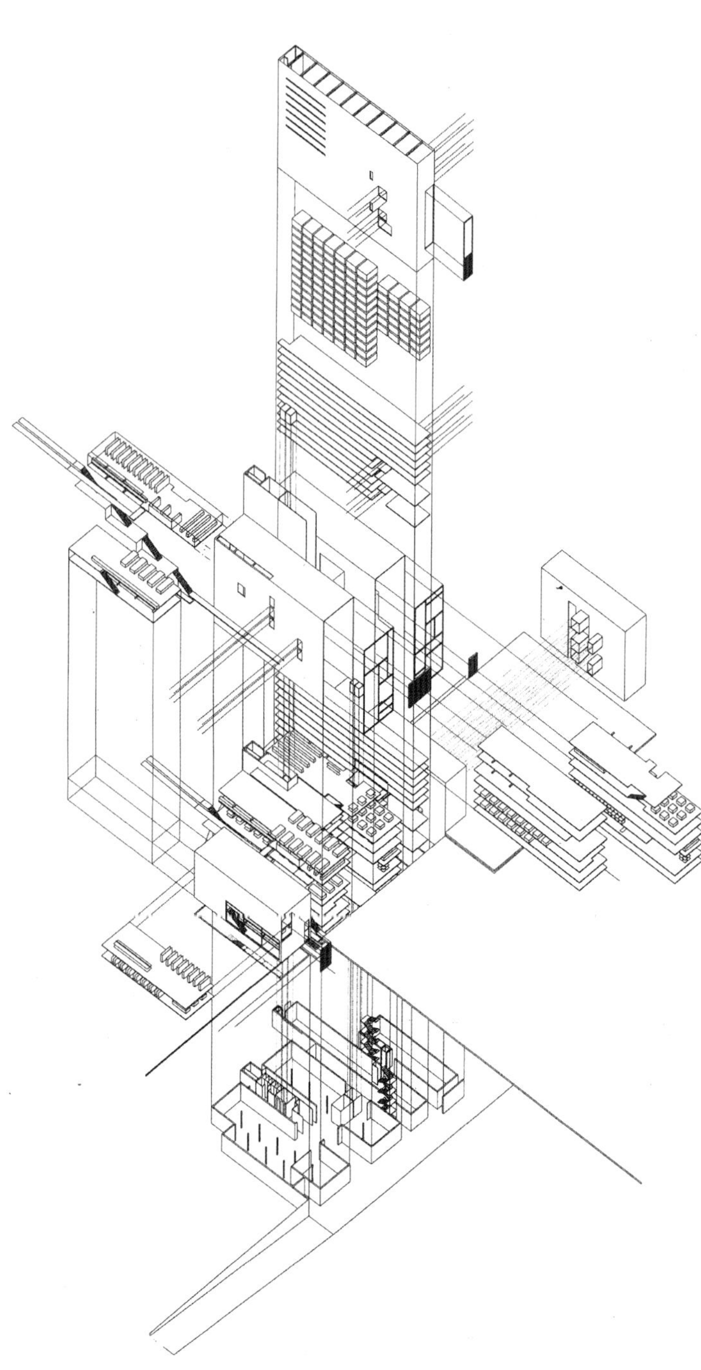

Exploded axonometric

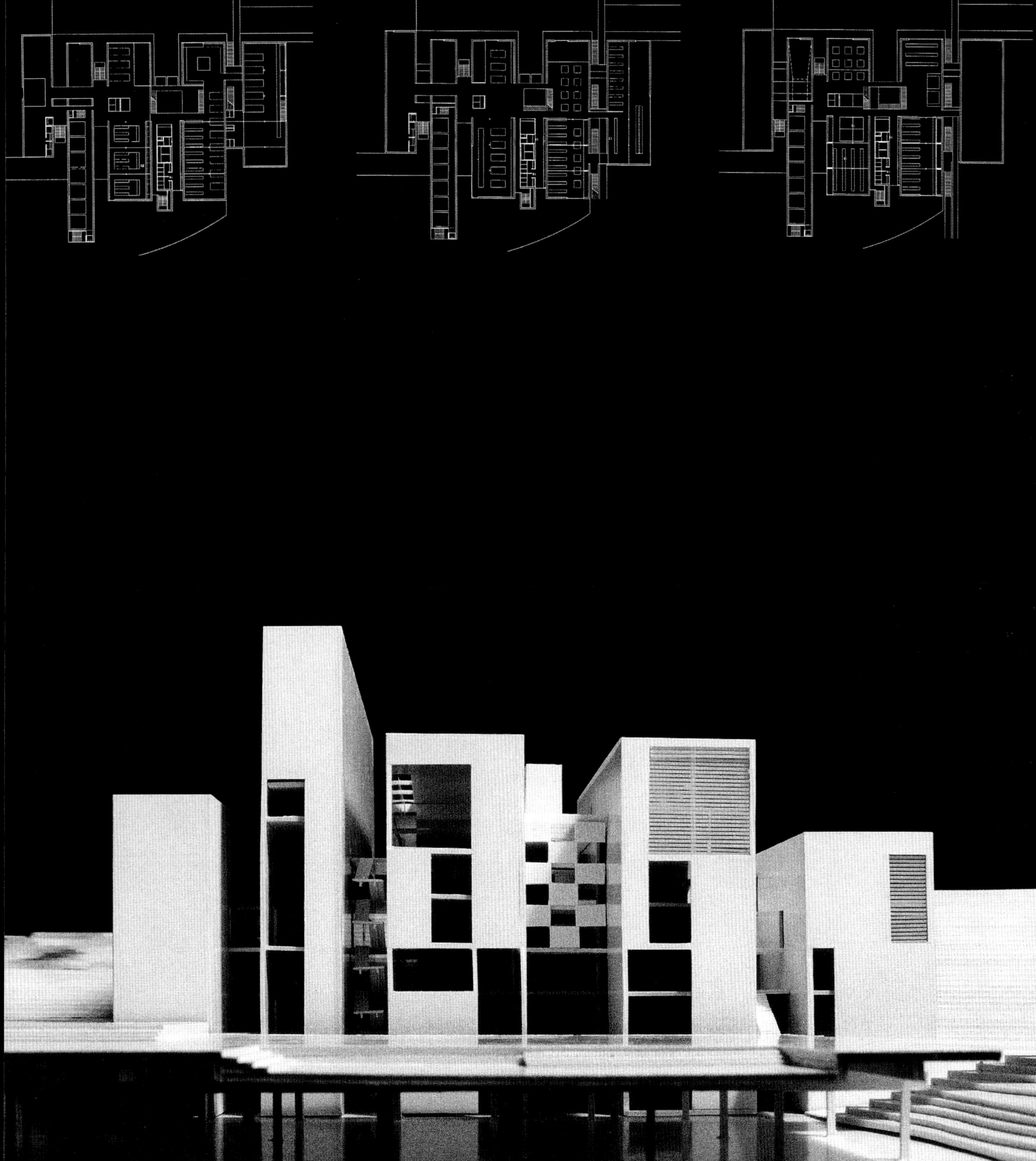

# Fitness Center. 1995

The idea of building underground was born from the urban impossibility of building above ground.

The building penetrates in the subsoil seeking some ancient foundation slabs at a depth of 7 m.

What at first glance appears as a set of walls, as a sculpture in the landscape, is revealed as false inside.

The false walls turn out to be large beams susceptible of spanning great lengths supporting the weight of the soil, achieving spatial transparency and helping to interconnect in the interior the different zones of the program.

The central courtyard, of small surface (somewhat more than 100 $m^{2)}$, is conceived in the form of star. This permits on one hand, to make light penetrate in-depth thanks to its long arms, and on the other, the concealment of its layout that hinders the perception of its scale.

The building is built with only one material - reinforced concrete - and travels the road of construction solely with the geometric order of the shuttering, with more care in the false walls, and rougher in the formation of the sloped slabs. A single constructive detail, the change in section of the lower level walls, which grow to form the screens that define the central space, allows the waterproofing and the formation of the reflecting pool.

The program is organised in two levels: an lower level contains the activities of more private character and the upper level, below ground but in touch with the garden through ramps that communicate it visually with the outside, contains all the proper activities of a centre of this type.

Finally, the building reveals itself as an underground box of light, which relates the internal space with the gardens outside, uses the light reflected from the pool, communicates visually the different spaces and protects them from external views.

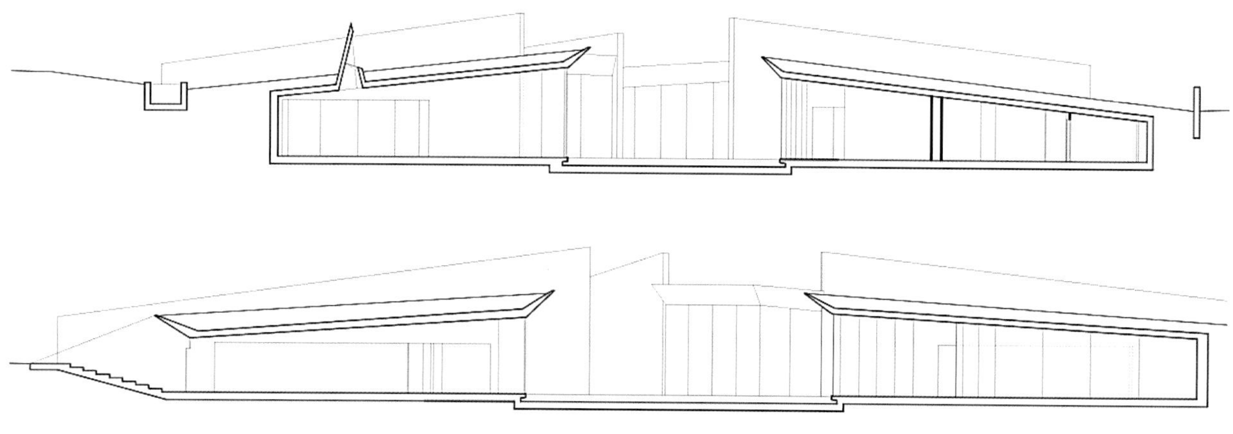


Sections

## Movie Studio. 1996

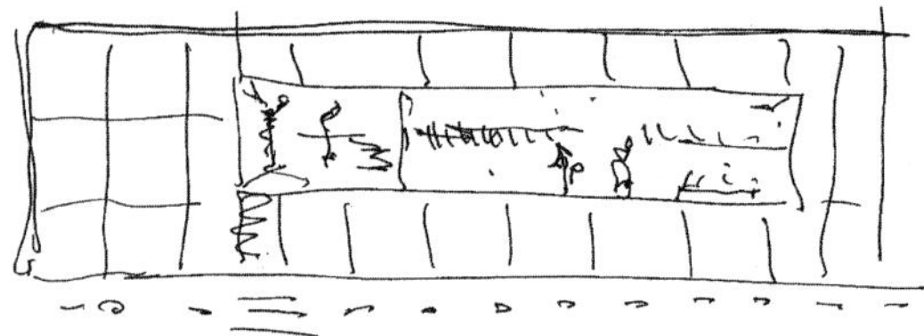

The project is born from the decision to locate the Arruga cinema studios in an industrial area of the periphery of Barcelona, considering movie and advertising production an industrial activity.

Thus, a building intended to harbour a creative activity, would have to co-exist in a grey and mute world - without language - of factories and stores with activity schedules typical of the industrial areas.

Because of the impossibility of generating a dialogue with its neighbours, the building becomes the image and the reflection of its own essence, thus showing itself in the only possible way: a building to make movies.

Its main façade becomes a piece of celluloid at night, converting into cinema the activity of the building itself: production, post-production, execution... with the rest of the program hidden behind the blind box: casting, wardrobe, attrezzo, stores, assemblies, workshops, dressing rooms and services, and finally the great space used as movie stage which presents itself in its most neutral form.

The construction, material, structure and facilities of this space are put to the service of the main activity reinforcing the neutrality of the project. The building is built with the technology and budget of an industrial warehouse: exposed steel structure with fires protection, deck floor slabs, concrete block walls, polished concrete floors, exposed services, façade of cement-wood boards.

The project incorporates a linear plantation of Populus Teixana, as an external element, close to the main facade.

This vegetation reveals a new interstitial space which is the negative of the interior. This space relates the internal activity with the outside space, and also uses its changing condition.

In summer a thick green mattress protects from the sun, in autumn it changes colour and purges its leaves, in winter it becomes a reflection on the large glazed window and in spring it shows its different colourings.

There is an open space intended for arrival and vehicles traffic between this tree screen and the street of the industrial area.

Finally, in an industrial area, a grey box poses an architectural issue: the relationship between the envelope and the internal space articulated by light.

# Open Geometries for mental landscapes

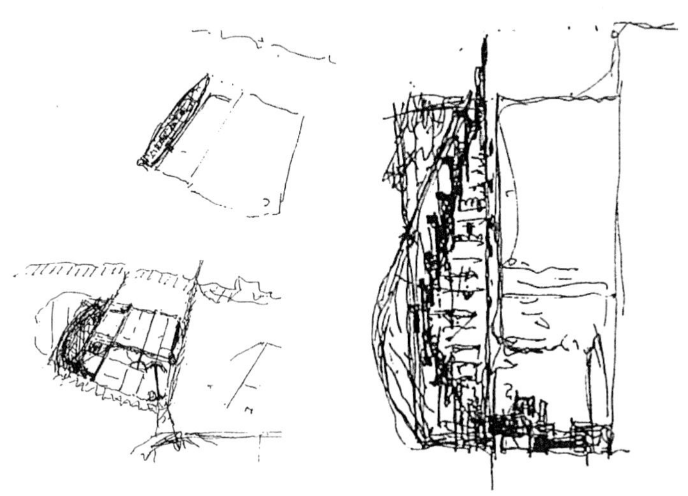

Site plan

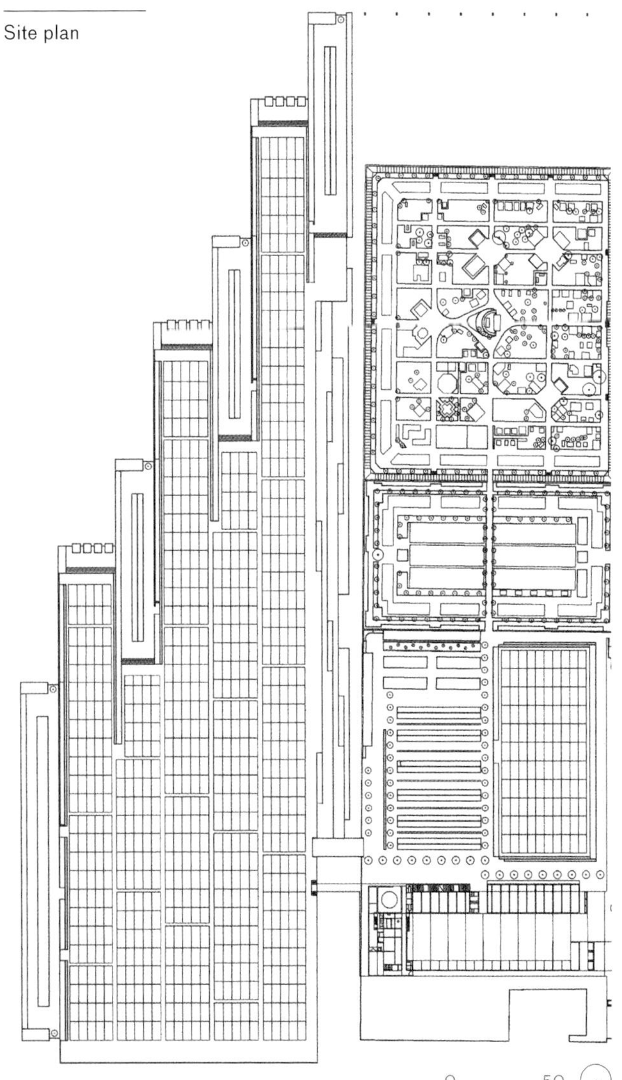


## Enlargement of the Cimitero di San Michele. Venice

*Isola senza tempo*

The project is linked to an idea of Venice and the surrounding area as the symbolic expression of the relationship between nature and artifice, and between the natural and man-made landscapes. It is the perfect expression of this because what was lacking at the beginning was the starting-point of every city: the earth between twvo surfaces having the same colour, water and sky. What was lacking was the spatial limit.

This complex relationship is amplified, becoming almost paradoxical, in the cemetery island because the nature-artifice duality is constructed to compensate for absence, far nothingness. With regard to this absence, almost as if by a quirk of history, some of the nineteenth-century maps did not even show the cemetery island.

If it were possible to think of the island without the phenomena around which it was farmed, its architectural significance would be reduced to the wall, the only constructed element that is itself an archetype of the enclosure - in other words, an instrument of the "architectural cultivation of the land".

If it is true that all the islands have a physiognomic identity, an individual character linked to their essence and a particular sense of time, because in the concept of the island the notion of waiting is intrinsic, then the cemetery island assumes the character of material and temporal absence.

## Musée des Confluences. Lyon

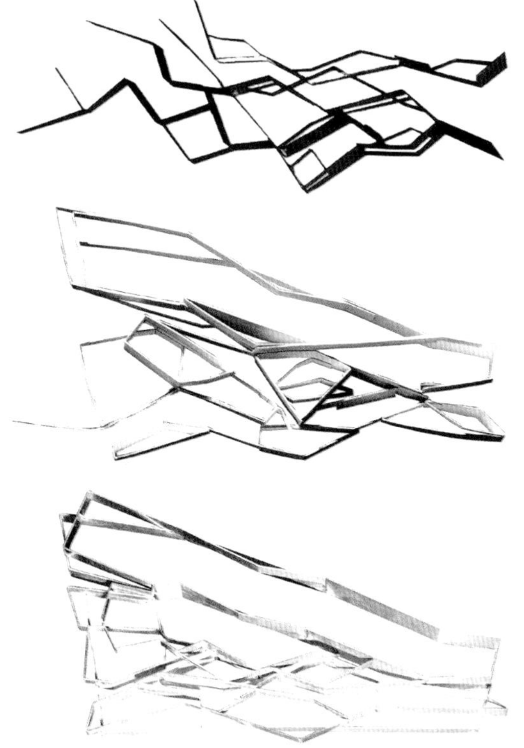

The location of the Confluence Museum of the Rhone and the Saone is landmark full of history. It occupies an important place in the imagination and identity of Lyon. Due to its symbolic role, and the place has become more a non-place, unused and lacking in quality.

The confluence of the Rhone and the Saona is marked by perpetual mutation. The beds of the river change over the centuries, first due to natural erosion and sedimentation, and other interventions produced by the man who seeks to dominate the rivers.

The project of the Museum offers the opportunity to build up the site to reflect its true image. Our proposal desires to monumentalize the place, instead of erase it behind a monumental building. The Museum is much more a symbol of the place than just an integral part of the site.

The volume of the museum is formed by a sequence of folded walls that intersect, separate, and create distance. These folds meet the conditions of the site, its symbolic role, its urban function and physical constraints, all while organizing the program and adopting structural solutions. It is a system capable of integrating all the complexity of the project.

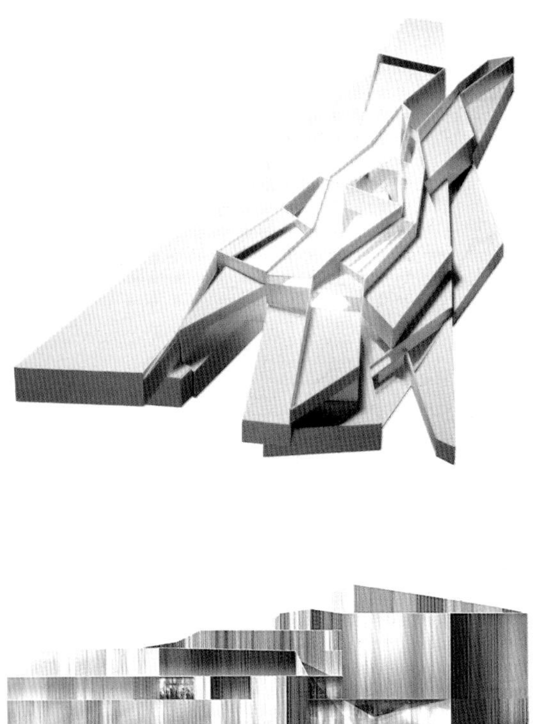

## Artabria Museum.
## Archaeological site. Galicia

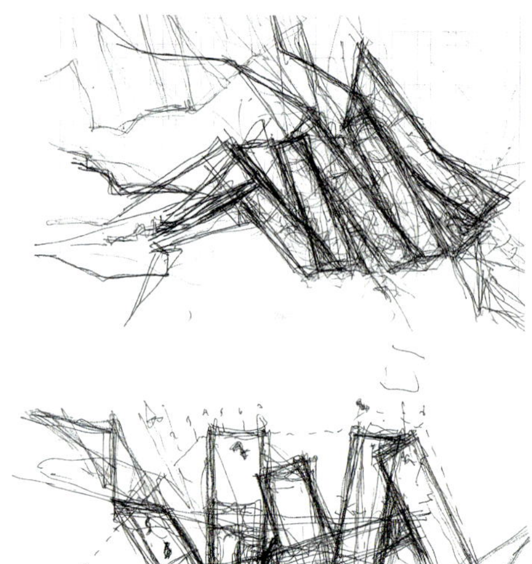

The proposal sites the museum in the area of intervention between the influence of the city and the hill fort, on the edge of the boundary of the park intended for the "History Center".

This is the place where the high-angle panorama of maritime La Coruña combines with the rooting to the "land" produced by the presence of the hill fort outline.

This geographical situation permits an itinerary for visiting the archaeological site to be constructed by rehabilitating stretches of the existing footpaths, the circuit being maintained in isotopic lines.

The building is a large porticoed structure incrusted in the north-facing hillside of Mesoiro. The part of this structure that is most underground is intended for the museum rooms, and the emergent part for the complementary program.

In terms of the topography, this layout creates a location that functions as an articulation between the archaeological site and the panorama of the city.

The building is designed as five big containers with a regular geometry (17 and 20 meters broad, repeatedly) that generate a "ribbon-like" museum circuit in the form of a zigzag some 375 meters long.

After passing through the seven museum rooms, the circuit winds down via a ramp that, going the other way, crosses these transversally.

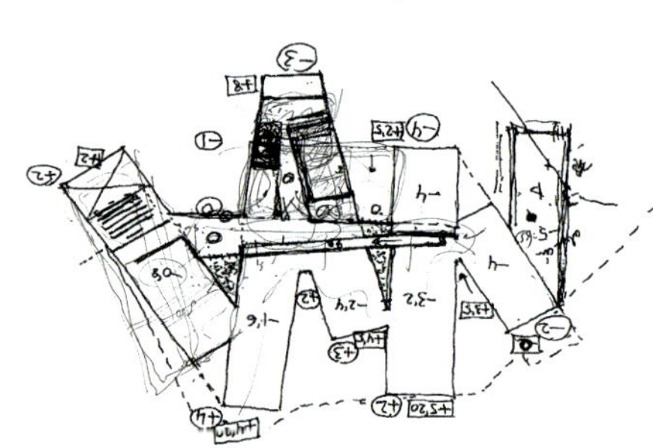

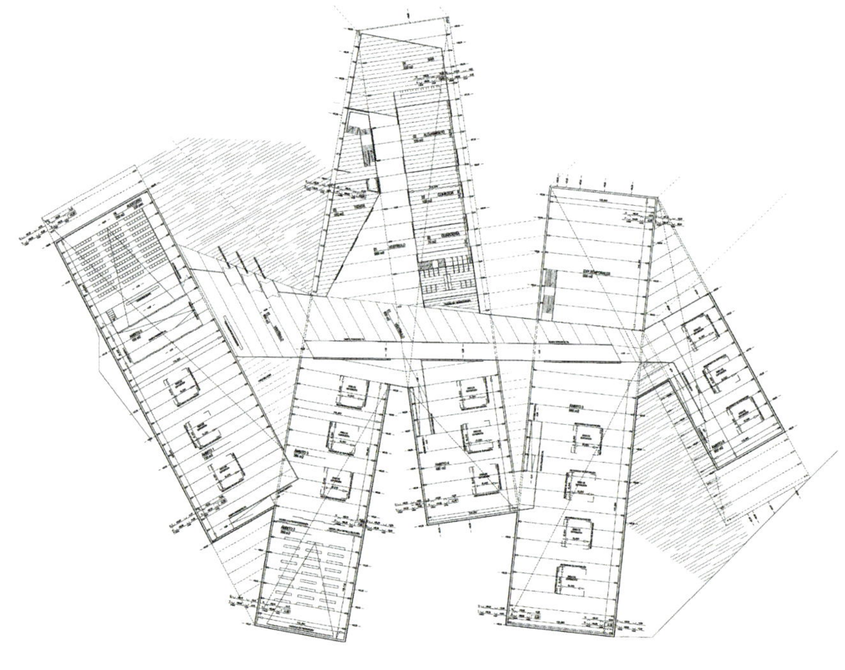


Ground floor

## Camp Nou Stadium. Barcelona

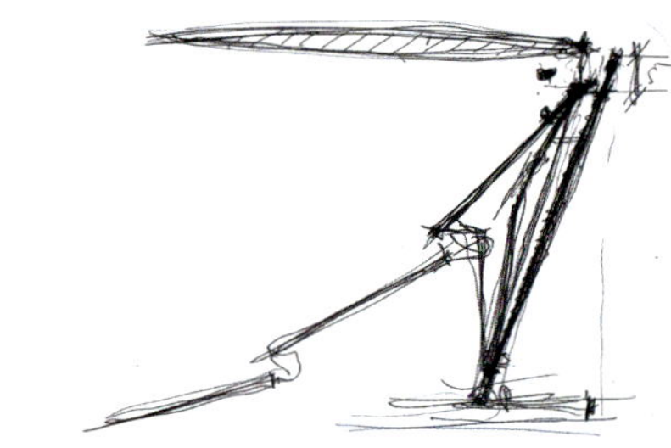

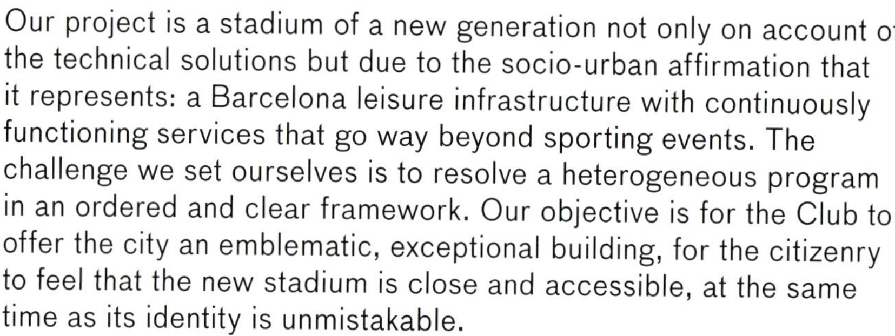

Our project is a stadium of a new generation not only on account of the technical solutions but due to the socio-urban affirmation that it represents: a Barcelona leisure infrastructure with continuously functioning services that go way beyond sporting events. The challenge we set ourselves is to resolve a heterogeneous program in an ordered and clear framework. Our objective is for the Club to offer the city an emblematic, exceptional building, for the citizenry to feel that the new stadium is close and accessible, at the same time as its identity is unmistakable.

The idea of remodeling Barcelona FC's stadium proceeds from maintaining the essential elements of the structure of the building that the architect Francesc Mitjans designed in 1957 as an original nucleus of the new project. Demolition of the more obsolete parts of the current stadium will permit the construction of a new seating tier, which, keeping to the layout of the original tiers, will complete the elegant interior bowl.

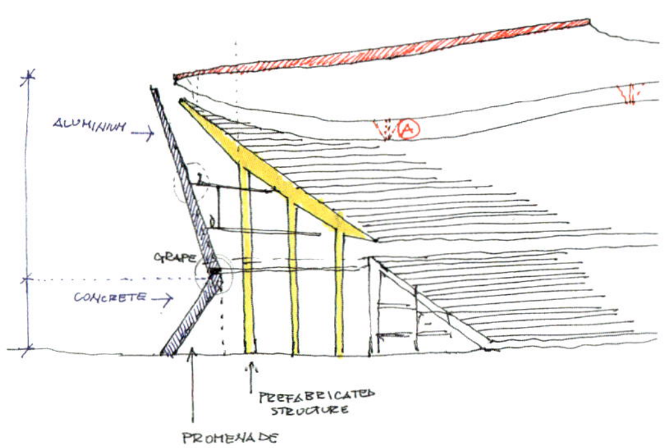


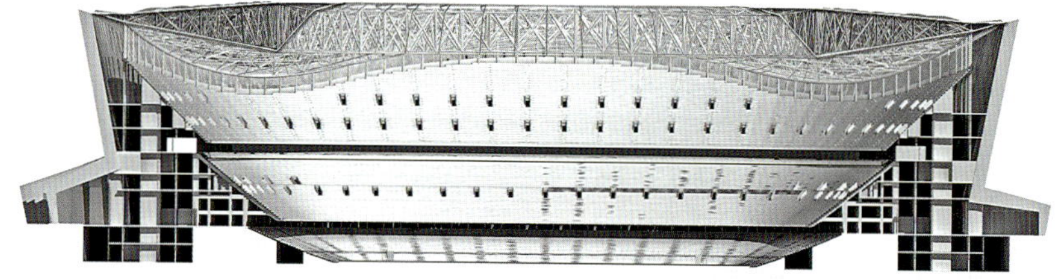

In order to have better visibility of the pitch it is necessary to concentrate the greatest number of seats in the bands parallel to its main axes and to reduce the number of seats at either end of the rectangle of play. This solution describes an elliptical shape in plan and a lightly undulating profile in section.

Designed on the basis of a sophisticated geometry, the roof will be resolved by means of the construction of a structure of intercrossing cables that reach their maximum section at two-thirds of the maximum span and which, meanwhile, are reduced towards the ends until arriving at a delicate slenderness. This is a system of easy and rapid execution, ideal for the circumstances of this project.

An ordered, profound and potent vertical rhythm of structural elements will cover the whole perimeter of the building, these elements being arranged according to the structural axes of the Mitjans opus as a peristyle, thus giving the stadium its unmistakable look.

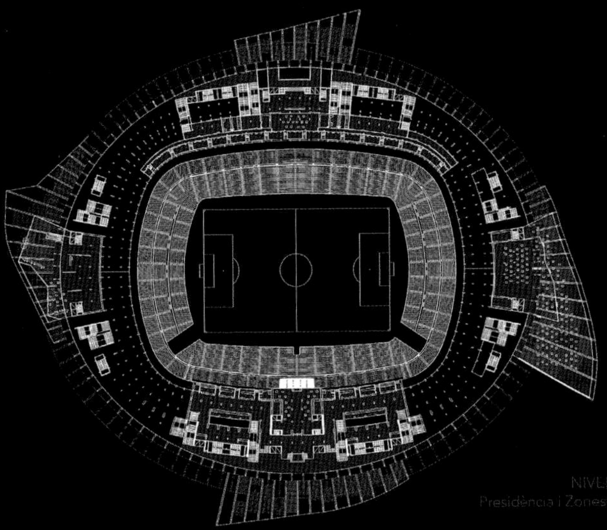

NIVELL 4
Presidència i Zones VIP

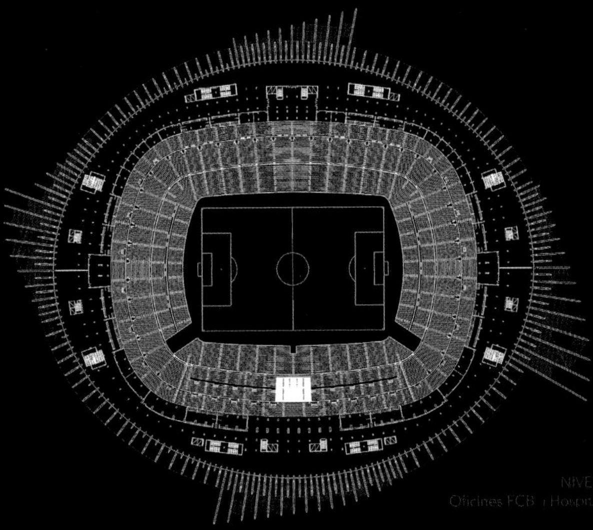

NIVELL 6
Oficines FCB i Hospitality

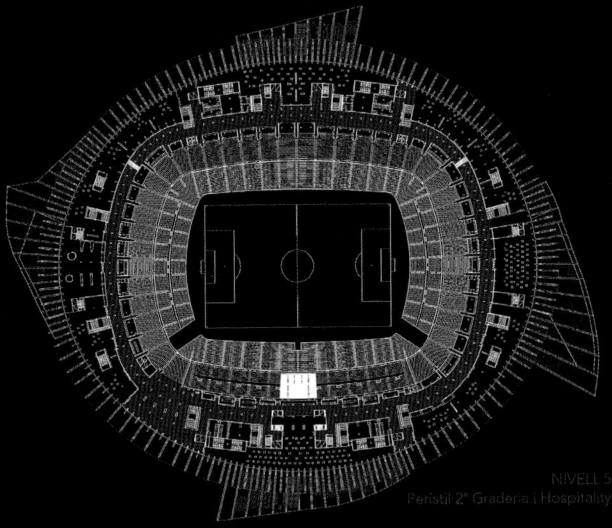

NIVELL 5
Peristil 2ª Graderia i Hospitality

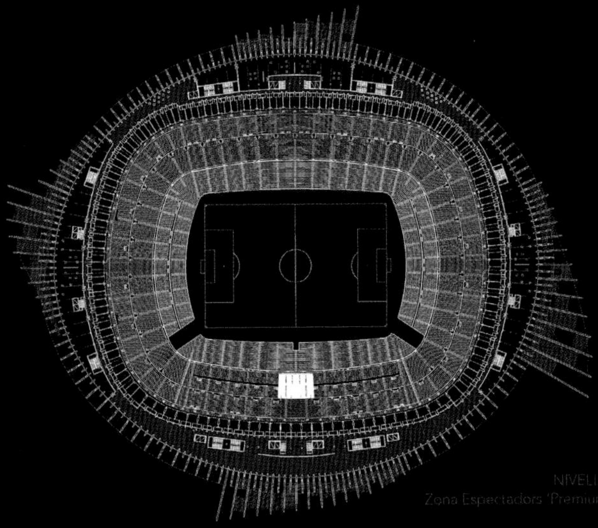

NIVELL 7
Zona Espectadors 'Premium'

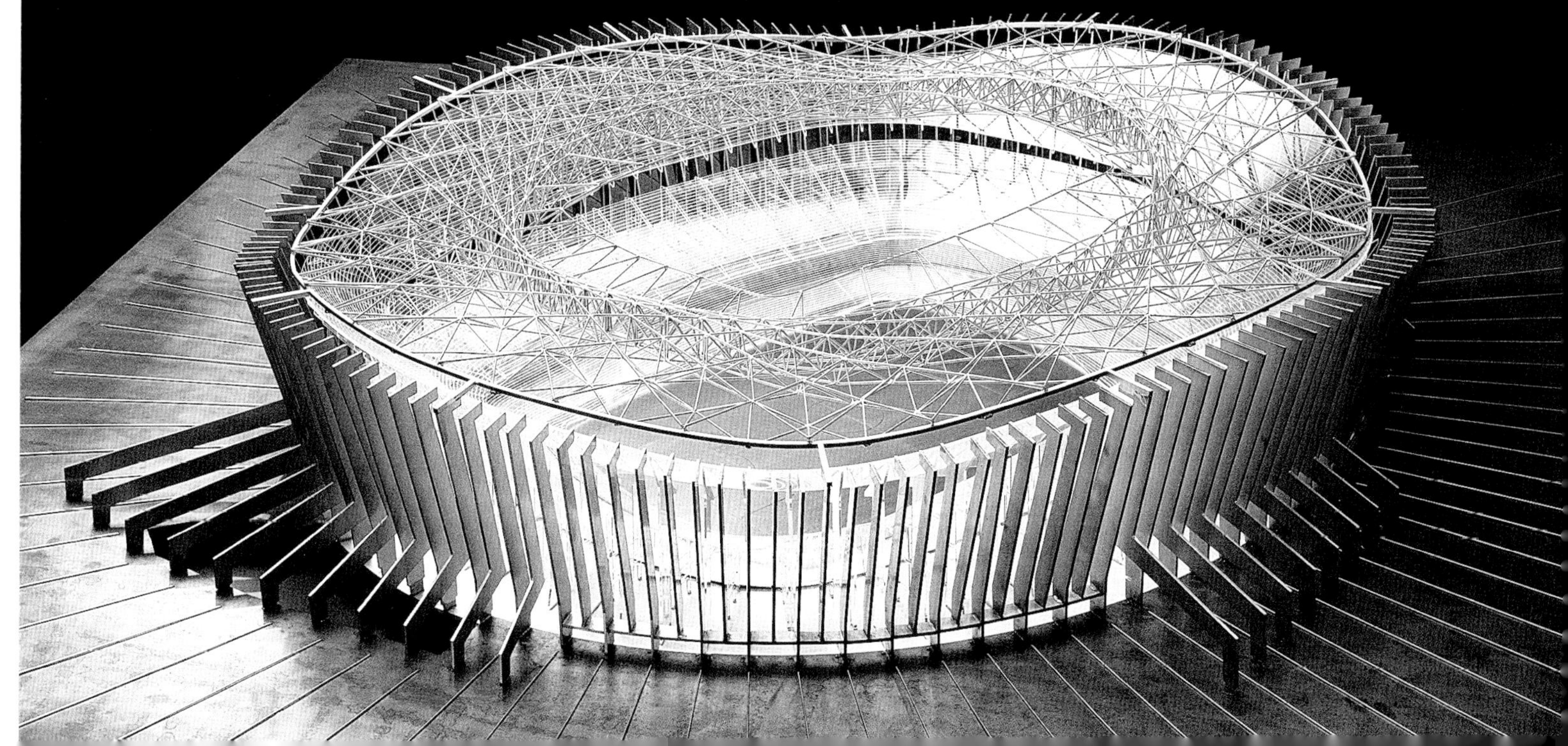

## Atapuerca milestone. Burgos

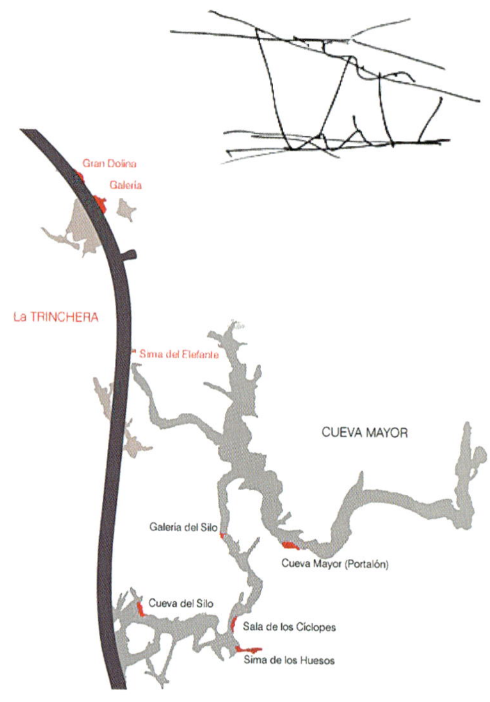


The Sierra of Atapuerca, located in the countryside bordering the city of Burgos, is recognized for the uniqueness and authenticity of its collection of fossils and stone tools used by the earliest known hominids in Europe. This location is registered as a Unesco World Heritage Site.

The project aims to unite two territories which run along a trench, 14 meters wide and 6 meters deep, where paleontological settlements are situated. Among them, the Gran Dolina of Atapuerca where Homo Antecessor (at least 900.000 years old), was discovered. It is considered the oldest known European hominid.

The program was developed around a bridge that incorporates a small reception pavilion, which interacts with an adjacent plaza embedded into the existing stone quarry. At this focal point of the project, the bridge integrates with the topography and landscape, preserving the visual, environmental and archaeological values of the site.

The bridge, as an extension of the roof, branches out into two separate arms, one leading into the building, and the other giving form and articulation to the building's structure. The building sits in between these arms, providing it with unrestricted access to daylight. These paths of circulation, although split, are still organized and interrelated by the direct relationship between visitor and researcher. One path is concerned with accommodating tourist visits and sightseeing, while the other path results from the research team of archaeologists. From a sustainable and inclusive viewpoint, the project reduces itself to basic parameters that are sensitive to the territory under study.

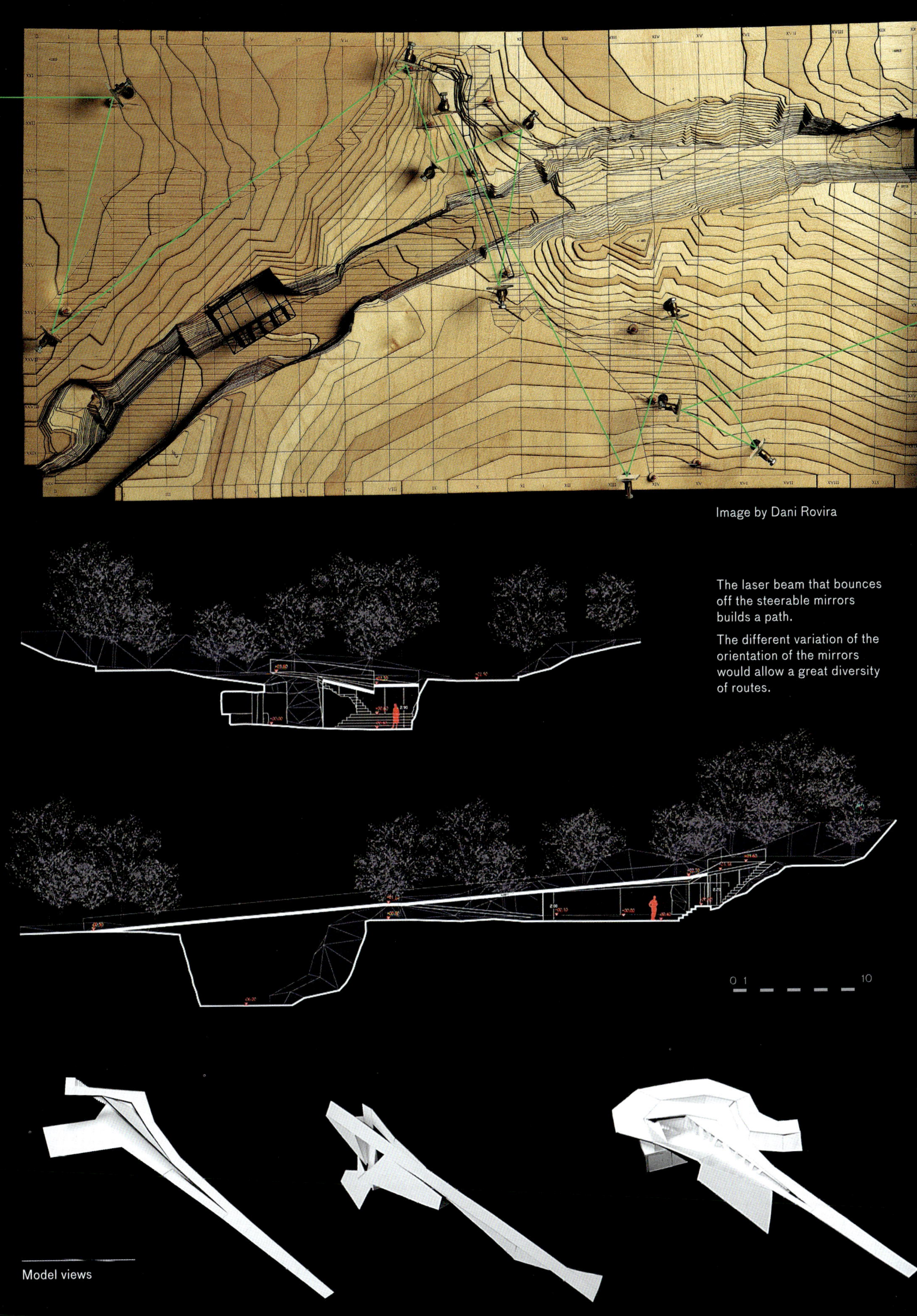


Image by Dani Rovira

The laser beam that bounces off the steerable mirrors builds a path.

The different variation of the orientation of the mirrors would allow a great diversity of routes.

Model views

# Urban laboratory

This chapter has been extracted from the monography "Carlos Ferrater" published by Actar. 2000

## New Diagonal

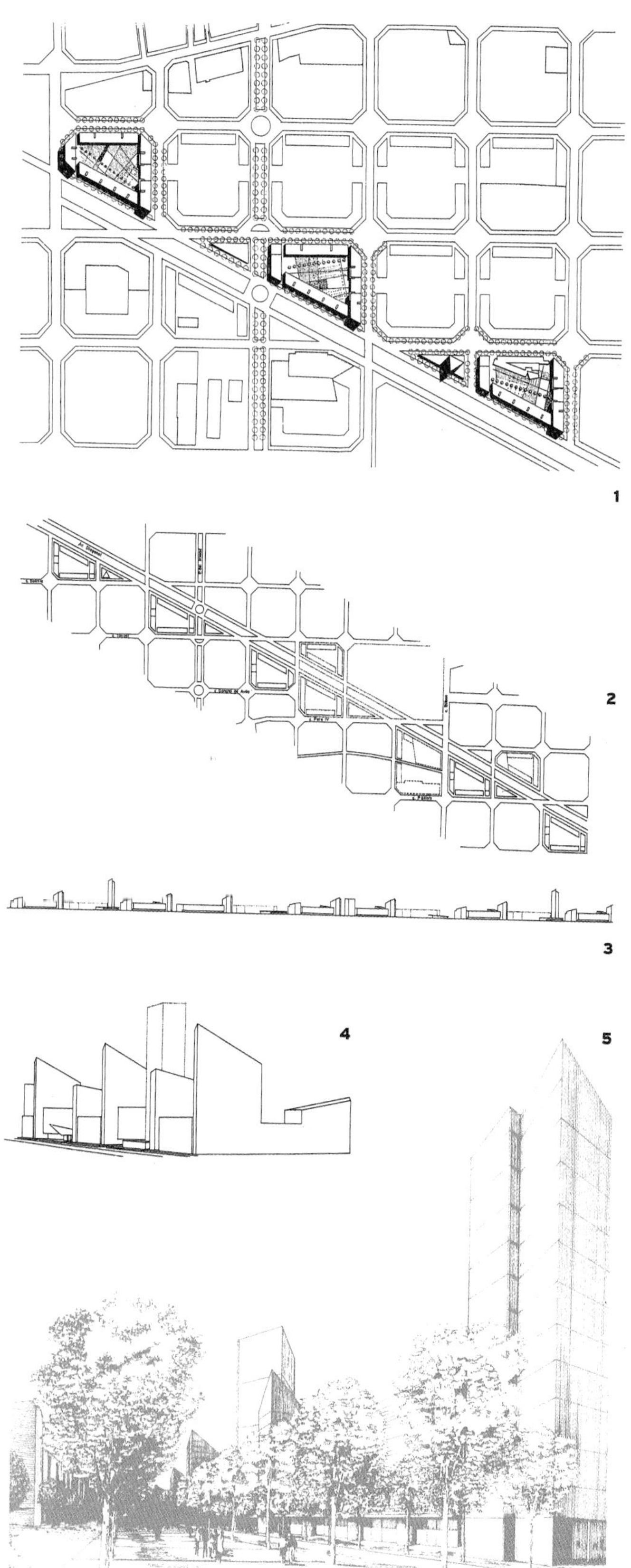

The contributions Carlos Ferrater has made to the field of forms of typological aggregation, to the development of the formal codes established by rationalism, plus the constant search for formal purification and precise execution are some of the themes most commented-on in relation to him. All these elements were already present in the first phase of his work and are also present in the current one, as can be seen in this book.

Perhaps the least-analysed aspects have had to do with urban interventions of a certain size in which, together with the specific discourse of the architecture, other extremely important projectural attitudes can be observed such as the success of a suitable project design at the urban scale. We might comment on three aspects arising in the design of urban entities of a certain size and of which, in the analysis of the work we are dealing with, it is important to single out the skill with which they are handled.

In the first instance, this entails looking at a number of the works from the viewpoint of what we take an urban project to be today, a that project whose architecture understands not only the building program but the one which stems from an attention paid to other urban variables present in the immediate context and which impinge on the project in a decisive manner. That in which the discourse of the architecture also incorporates other theses arising from the location and from those parameters the form of the city imposes.

In this case, this does not mean that schemes of a certain size have not been analysed or that the incidence of buildings or groups of buildings in public space has not been taken into account. Perhaps it is a question of looking at the ability to comprehend the overall context into which they are inserted and the facility to uncover the basic references of the environment, knowing how to set aside secondary questions in order to arrive at the essential factors of the structure and of the urban fabric in which one works.

Secondly, the author's work in what has been called the mid-scale must be noted. This is the name given to those schemes which develop parameters and guidelines of a generally abstract planning kind, actualizing them in terms of urban form yet without managing to become a constructional project in the strict sense. This is a work of approximating to the urban form in which highly important projectural decisions are taken, such as the systems of morphological aggregation, the nature of public spaces, the typological verification of functional programs and references to the context. In such cases the main focus of attention has to be on the aspects cited above, since they will be the ones which sustain the projectural idea that other architects may perhaps develop. Working at this scale

**Proposal for a block scheme in the New Diagonal**
1989. Barcelona. With Josep M. Montaner

**1** Plan of the new Diagonal scheme
**2** General layout
**3** New Diagonal elevation
**4** Volumetry of typical block
**5** Visualization from the avenue

# Poblenou Seafront

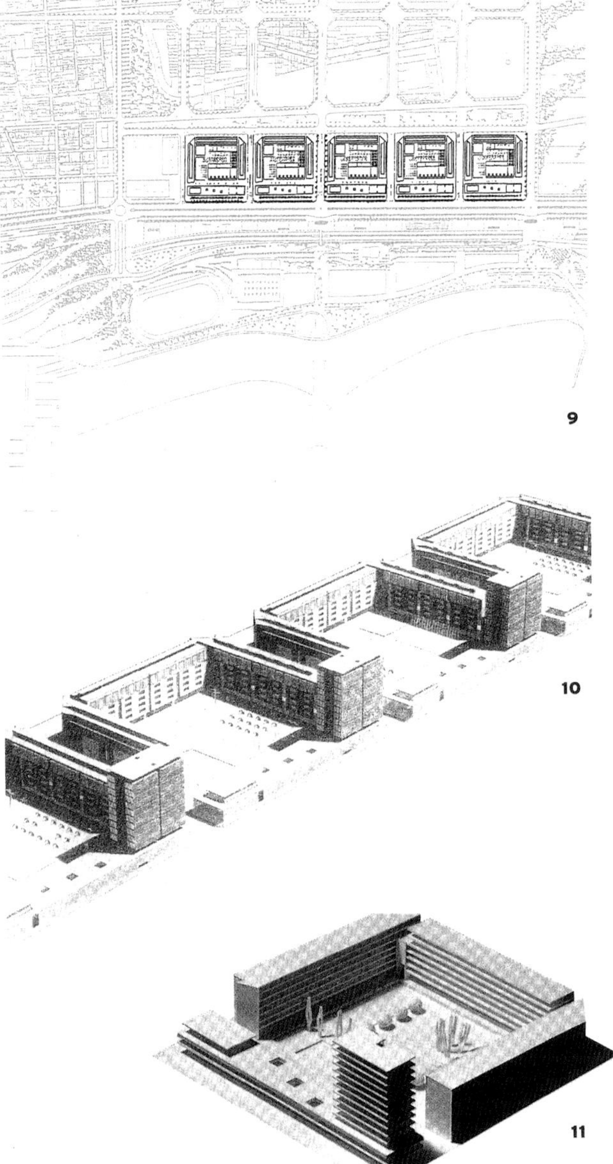

9

10

11

itself, at least a critical discussion of that model. In the last two cases this is by the interstitial, or if you like, border effect which largely conditions any solution that strives for suitable imbrication in the urban situation.

Of the three schemes for the Eixample, one responds to a uniformly executed project for a single operator: the three Poble Nou blocks. The other two are more general developments that emerged from a consultation at the request of the Town Council with various architects.

These last fall within the mid-scale works mentioned above, inasmuch as the mass is broken down for implementation in independently projected block-sized units.

An attitude similar to Cerdà's initial idea subsists in these three cases.

The attitudes of the architects have been different in the Eixample interventions. A first group argues for respecting certain basic ideas on which the extension planned by Cerdà is based: the grid of streets with their interaxial dimensions, and the section of the streets; supplementing the characteristics of the constructed extension: edification at roof height and in the higher parts of the buildings to around 6 or 7 stories in height.

A second focus would be one which attempts vaster kinds of aggregation, maintaining the road grid but varying the scale of the urban form, as in the case of the GATCPAC schemes for Barcelona or the Olympic Village in which the buildings that configure the superblocks pass above the streets and their interiors accommodate semi-public spaces or even low-density urban fabrics. Or recent schemes for open-ended development, realized, in fine, during the consultation for the five seafront blocks previously cited, in which, based on solid reasons of urban positioning, it was proposed to handle the development of the seafront at a much greater scale of edification and composition.

Finally, we encounter alternative options to the morphology of the city block, which include a number of interesting theoretical exercises devoted to the Cerdà block.

12

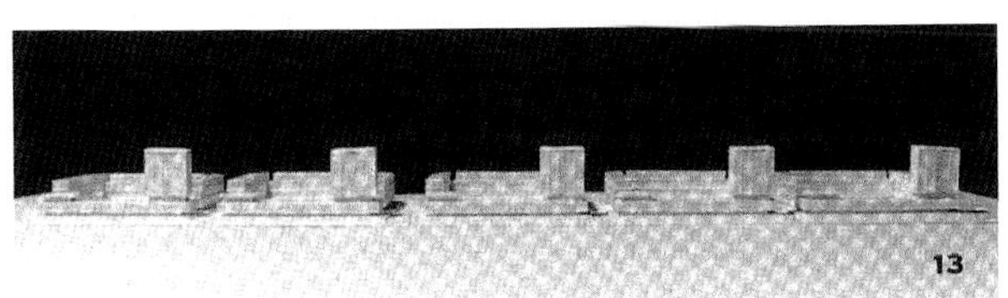

13

**Proposal for five blocks in the Poble Nou Seafront**
1995. Barcelona. With J.M. Montaner

**9** General location of the five blocks, from the promenade
**10** Rendering of the scheme
**11** Model of typical block
**12** Initial sketch
**13** Model of the five blocks

# Foix Avenue

A similar issue is tackled in the Avenida Foix, although it's clear here that the terrain worked on is obviously an interstice between the old area of Sarrià and the residential garden-city neighborhoods of recent times.

Like many older neighborhoods which were once municipalities and independent nuclei within the Barcelona plain, Sarrià has possessed a clearly defined internal structure that becomes imprecise at its perimeter. Many streets forsook their continuity, the limits of the traditional fabric were ambiguous and there were even de-urbanized areas existing on the course of old streams which rendered its urbanization difficult.

The Avenida Foix project is situated in one of the latter areas, with the laying out of a new road system envisaged – and since built – which has resolved the linkage with one of the exits from the Ronda de Dalt and also defined the western edge of the Sarrià neighborhood.

Once again the solution adopted responds to a whole having two faces: one which now follows the layout of the new avenue, and the other which allows for integration with the Sarrià neighborhood, adapting the volumes and planning to its scale and geometry.

The continuous curve of the avenue's main building contrasts with the irregular outline of the lower block in the interior street, with its length and the orientation of its end-walls being limited in order to provide an exit for the streets of the Sarrià web.

Neither is the siting ignored of open spaces of restricted dimensions but enormous efficacy, given the size of the built mass and the scale of the neighborhood.

The two works could be defined as attempts at urban 'finish'. Independently of the merit of their architecture or the success of their language, it is certain that there is an awareness of the urban role they must play and, as we said at the beginning, of their incorporation in formal decisions about the urbanistic needs of the context.

The group of projects analysed provides an example of the best road to follow for medium-size urban interventions in terms of focus, method and results, and once the objective of the city's recomposition is added to the individual architectural solution.

Many architects and their work have contributed to the definition of what has been called the 'Barcelona model'. As can be deduced from this commentary on a part of his oeuvre, the projectural attitude of the author has been an important contribution to the formulation of that model.

**Ricard Fayos** Director of Urban Planning Services of the Ajuntament de Barcelona. Professor of Urban Planning in the ETSA of Barcelona

34

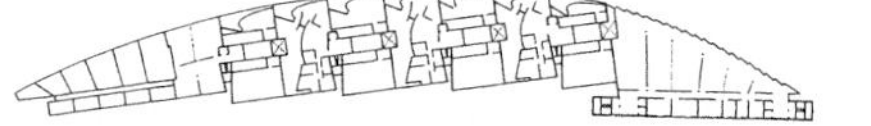

35

**Housing building**
1991–1996. Avenida Foix. Barcelona. With José M. Cartañá

**32** Pre-1990 situation
**33** 1993 situation, with urbanization
**34** Basic floor plan
**35** Detail plan
**36** Finalized intervention of the housing complex between Sarrià and Pedralbes

36

# Between centuries 1998–2004

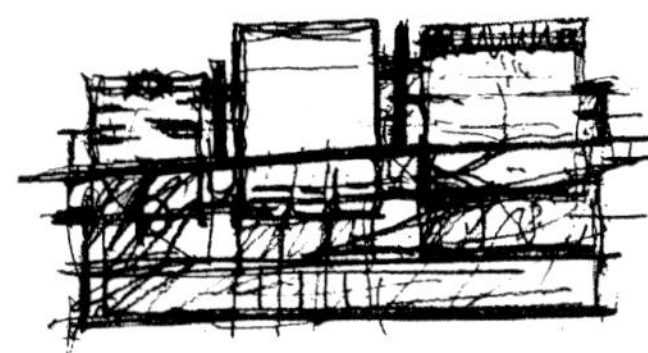

## Catalonia Convention Center

The Palau de Congressos de Catalunya (Catalonia Convention Center) stands in the southwest limits of the city of Barcelona and presents its two main facades into the gardens of Torre Melina and Avinguda Diagonal.

This is, then, an entrance point to the city of Barcelona with a large concentration of university, sport, financial, commercial and hotel amenities. Avinguda Diagonal is a street which offers a wide range of hotels.

The building is divided into three volumes separated by the site's own two streets providing visuals communication between Avinguda Diagonal and the gardens of La Torre Melina, and allowing daylight into its rooms. These lengthwise streets dividing the complex into lengthwise strips are joined by the hall, the foyer and crosswise elements: the two streets at garden level which lead into independent, complementary entrances.

The centre is laid out not so much in the form of independent functional elements as with a social system of overlapping parts which to make up a kind of mini-city.

The circuit starts in the hall, continues along the street before entering the main auditorium with capacity for over two thousand people and into the foyer, which is a place rather than a container for activity, due to the imposing presence of the landscape. The exhibition hall also stands out for its identifiable exterior image and the way light is treated. From here on, the circuit continues through the lower floor on a level with the gardens; this floor contains the modular halls, dining rooms and a series of support services including the cafeteria-cum-restaurant, offices and complementary spaces corresponding to the third sector of the building. The complex functions as an interwoven system, as a whole in the form of a kind of small city.

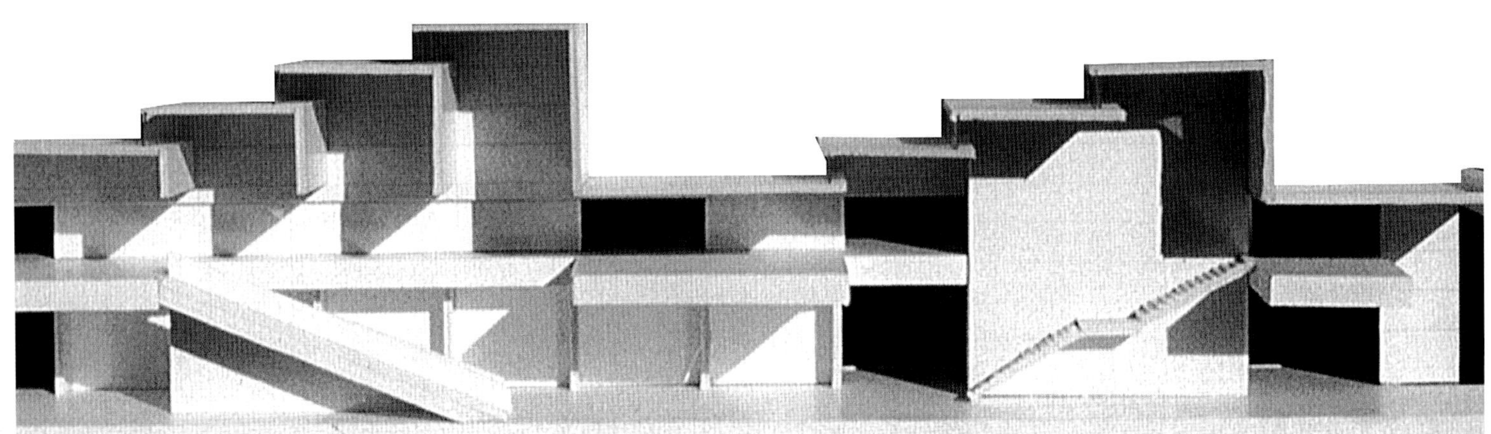

Section model

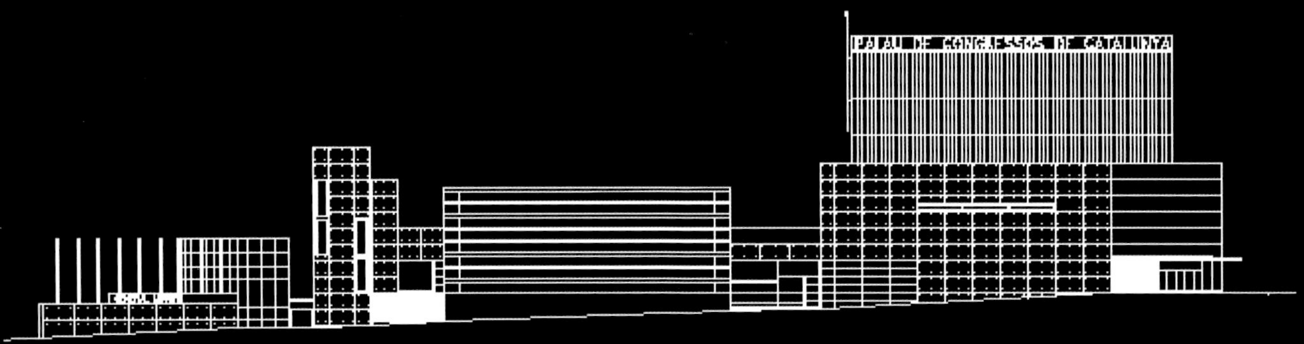


North and south elevations

PALAU DE CONGRESSOS DE CATALUNYA

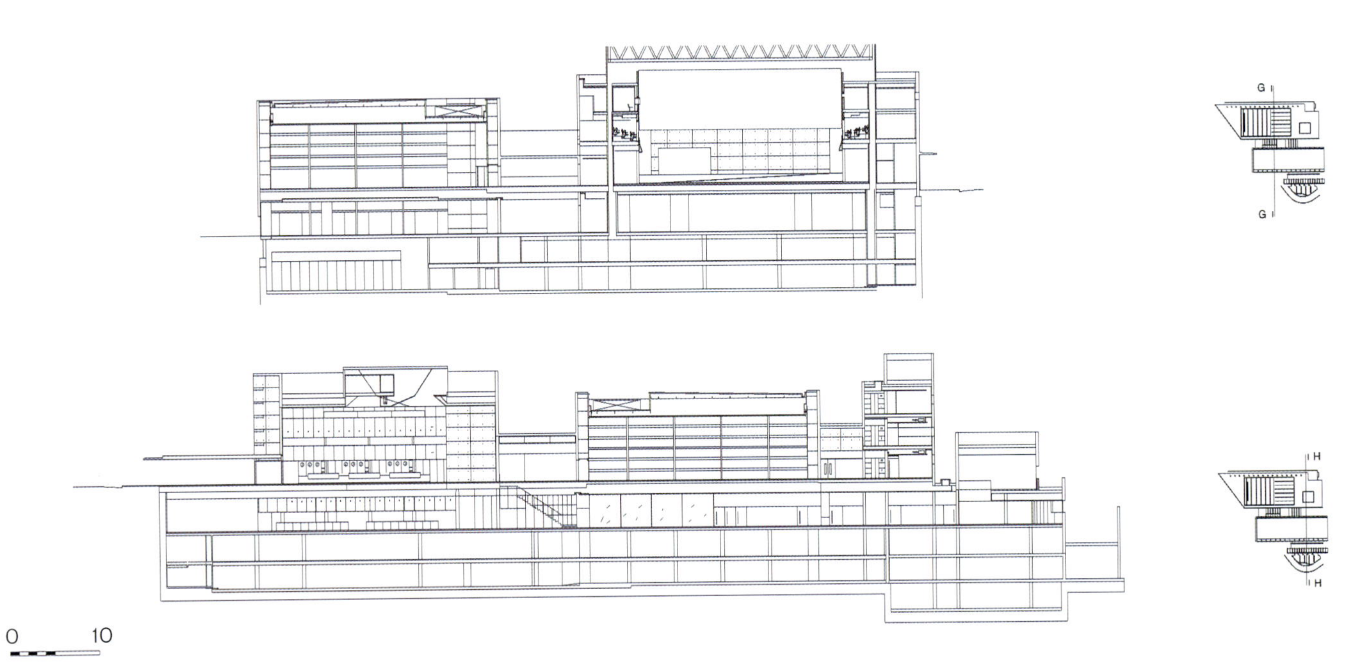


Sections

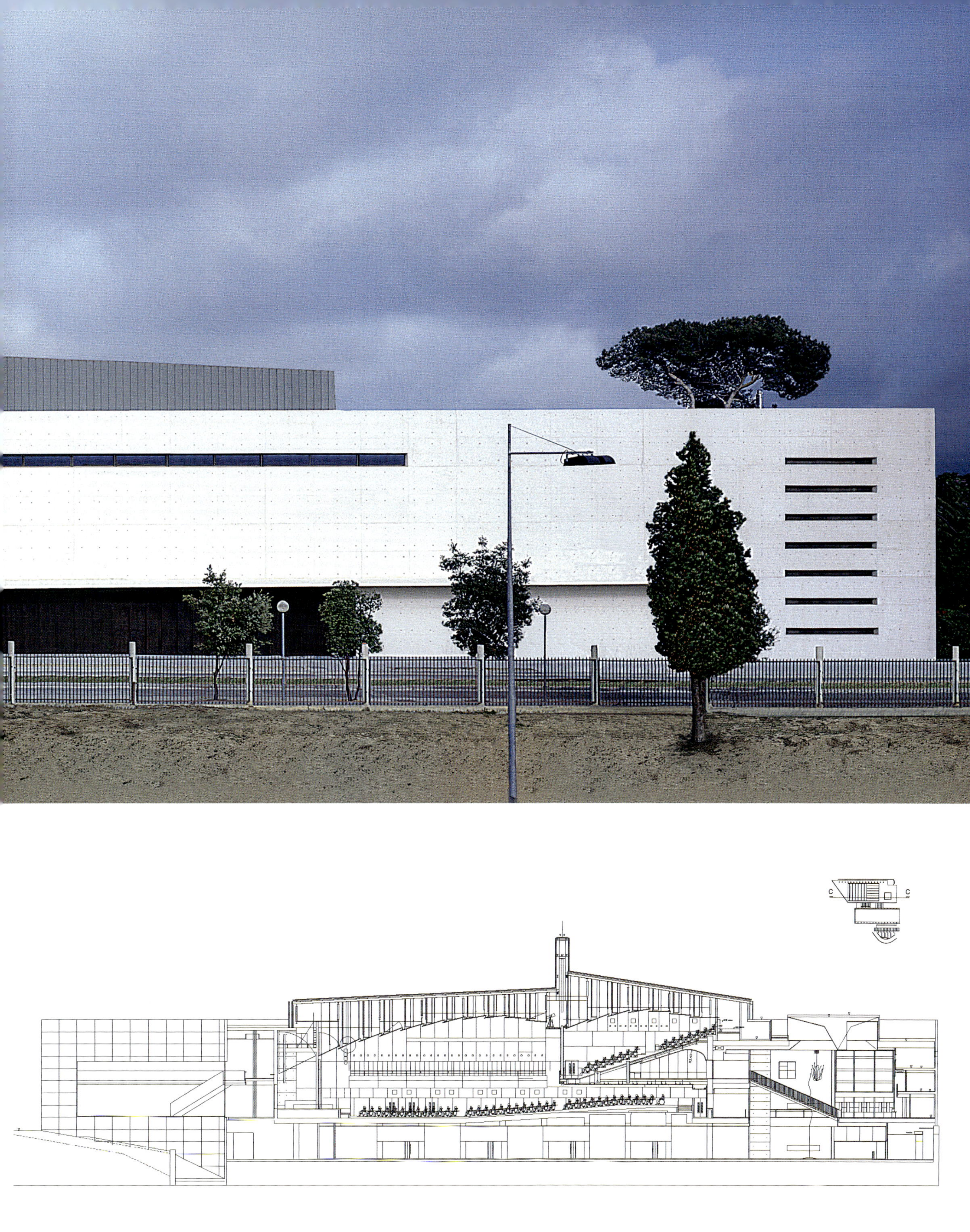

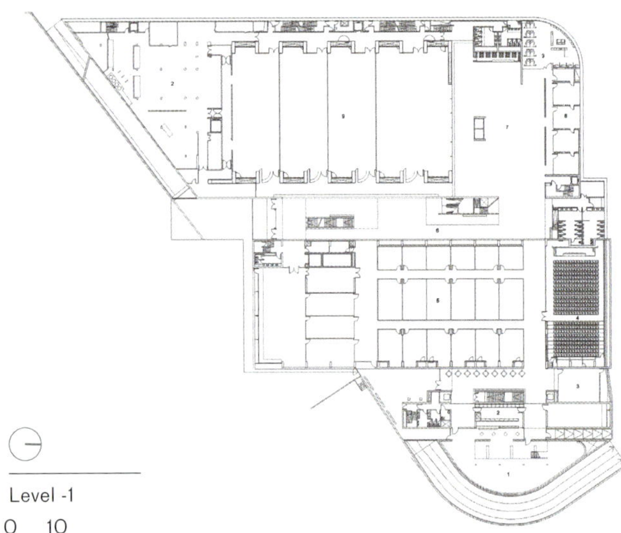

Level -1

0 10

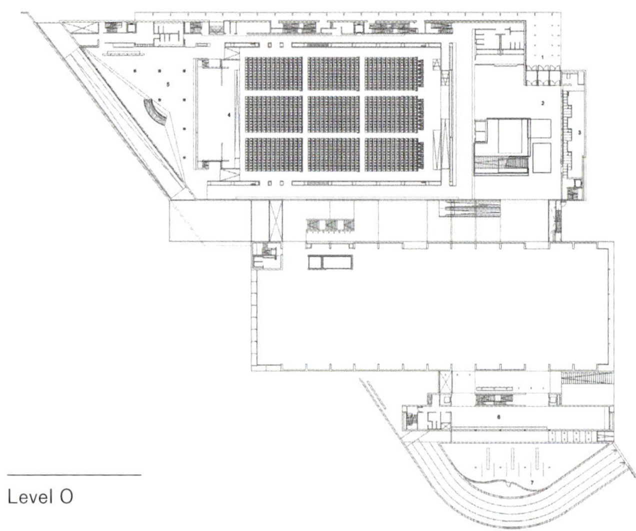

Level 0

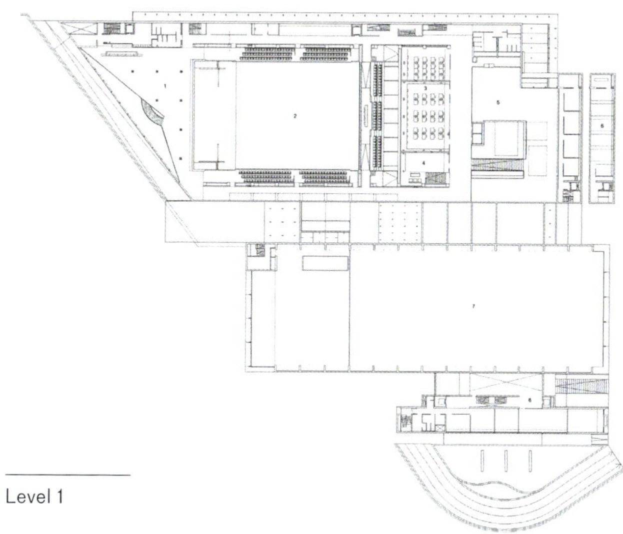

Level 1

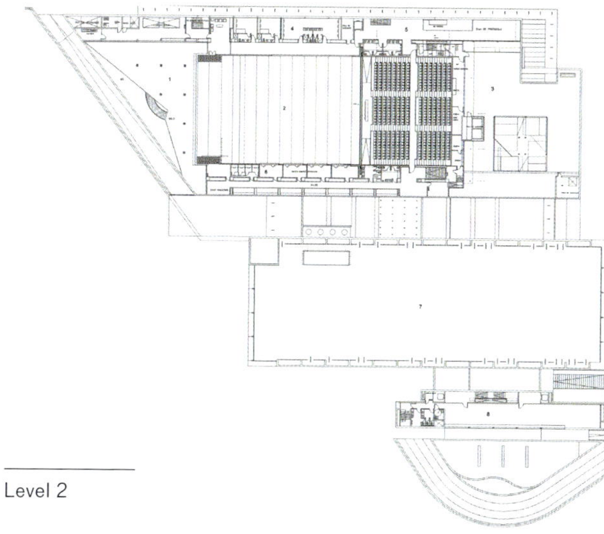

Level 2

## International JC Decaux Headquarters

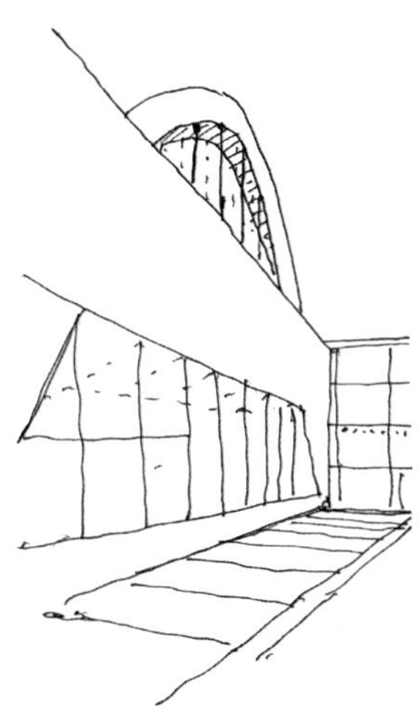

The new head office of the street-furniture company International J.C. Decaux occupies the one-time building of the former Martini & Rossi factory, a building from the early 1960s created by the architect Jaime Ferrater in an industrial area on the outskirts of Madrid. The complex is protected by the Architectural Heritage Law and consists of a huge vaulted hangar with a structure of arches, a body intended for the administration department, and a series of warehouses and service areas, the expression of a truly contemporary poetics of tremendous formal elegance.

The project thus confronts a topical issue and rehabilitates the architecture of that time with a sense of deep respect for what already exists, bearing in mind its objective architectonic quality. In that sense, a series of non-invasive architectural interventions are undertaken, interventions suited to adapting the building to the requirements of its new user. The project is mainly centered on three intervention criteria:

– While respecting its original language, to rehabilitate the facade

– The new use of the space, intended as an administrative headquarters as well as a display area for the street furniture produced, plus the need for a series of spaces open to the public.

– The internal structure is absolutely respected.

The new entrance irrupts into a triple-height lobby, the communications nerve center of the building. From this concourse we accede to the offices occupying the original administration building of the large roofed hangar with its arch structure (the former Martini & Rossi bottling area), adapted as a showroom for street furniture, and to the space intended for receiving clients and visitors, which has a small conference room and a double-height cafeteria giving onto a patio-cum-garden.

The larger garden at the rear is seen to be a more intimate space than the one the offices enjoy.

Pre-restoration status

Martini & Rossi Opening party.
Architect: Jaime Ferrater

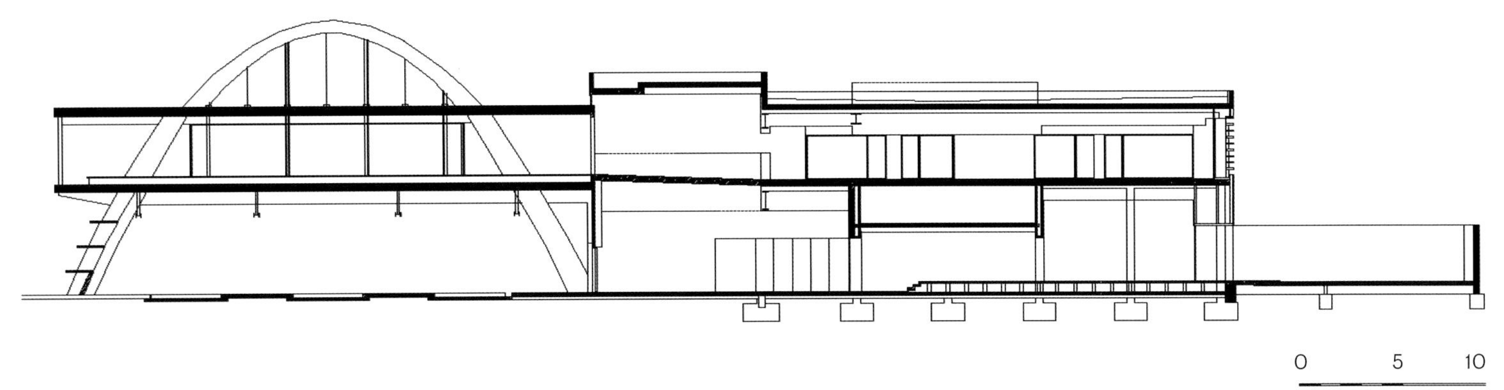


Cross Section

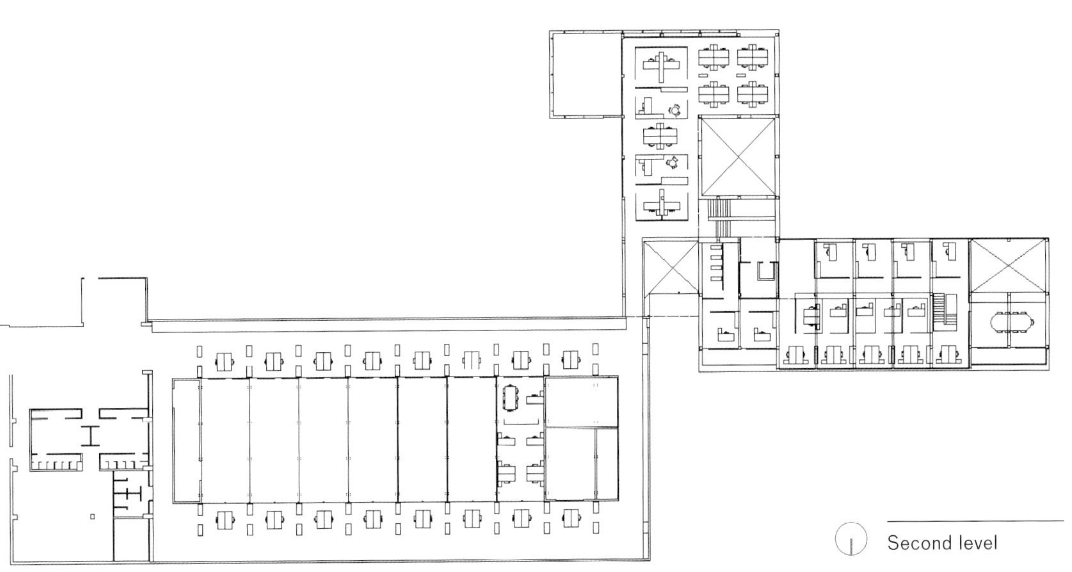

Second level

## Social Services Center

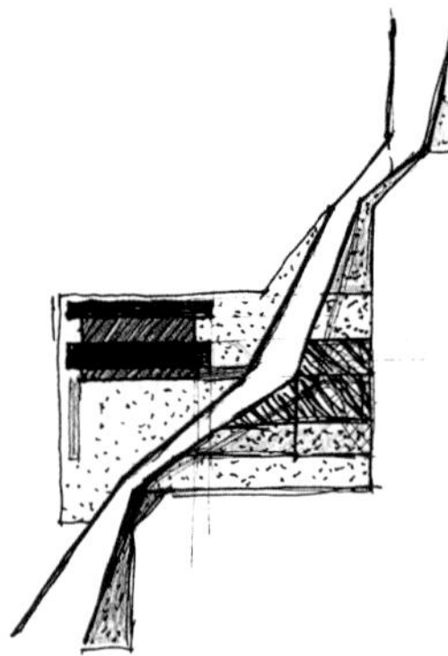

The building is located in a specially designed public space within a city block that reaffirms the layout of the old Horta road.

The main façade is orientated towards the southeast, allowing a clear view to be had from Calle Alibei, where the southern access of the garden is located. This is organized in a set of bands which define the different leisure areas by using different kinds of paving.

The units that form the building increase and decrease in size according to the light that falls upon the spaces inside. The varying lengths of the different areas leads to the appearance of two patios at the ends, which play their part in the lighting and ventilation while being more closed in towards the outside.

This idea is reinforced by the building components used: plain concrete, glass in the patios and skylights, lattice-like perforated aluminum, and zinc on the roof, which emerges as a fifth façade.

A group of residential buildings on Carrers Alibei, Roger de Flor and Nàpols rounds off the intervention.

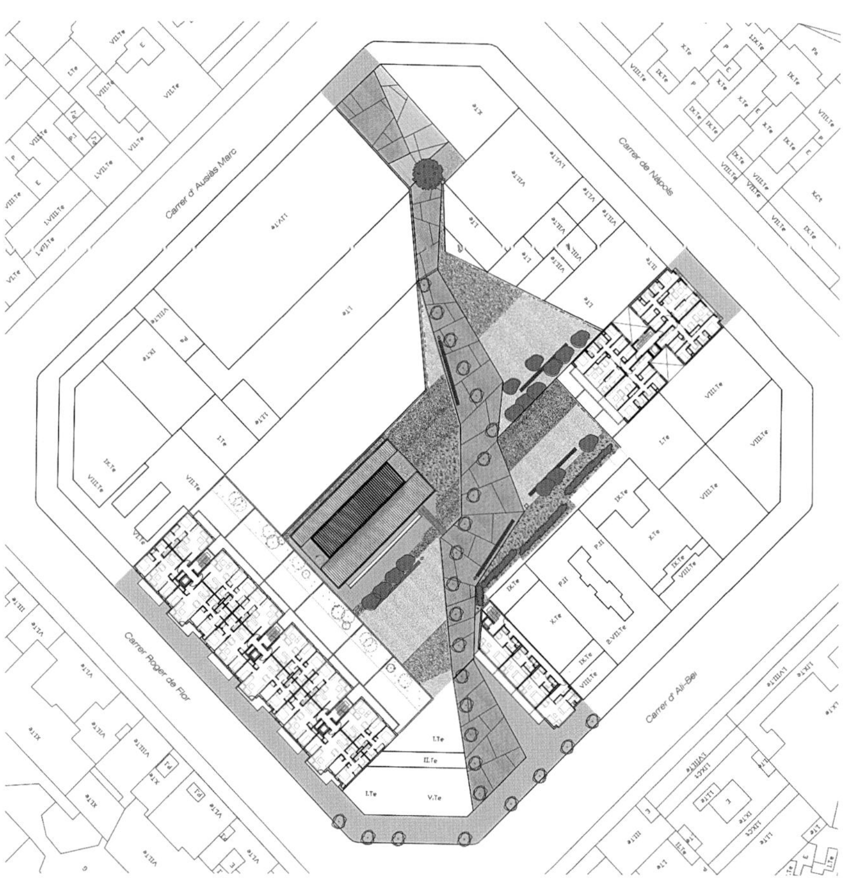


*"This intervention by Carlos Ferrater and Lucía Ferrater presents a model for rehabilitating the blocks of Barcelona's nineteenth-century urban grid, the interior courtyards of which have been largely taken over by industrial use. The architects created a diagonal path that leads from two external corners of the block through to new public gardens and a social services center located in the internal court. Private housing units are inserted into the blocks perimeter. Landscaping in the central gradens was designed in long modules, creating distinct zones for children's play, specific plantings, and other elements. The center is integrated with the garden, using the same modular system to differentiate various programs within the building. A central clerestory creates a light-fileled interior. Combining public and private interests, the project facilitates the redevelopment of community space within the city grid. "*

**Terence Riley, MoMA Chief Curator**

**On-Site: New Architecture in Spain 2006 Exhibition**

Site plan

0 5 25

Nàpols 81

Ali Bei 38

Roger de Flor 82

Interior of the island that recalls the old road that, in the 19th century, connected the walled Barcelona with Horta, traversed by porters, laundresses and tartans of the nobility and that can be remembered in this courtyard of the island.

# El Prat Royal Golf Club

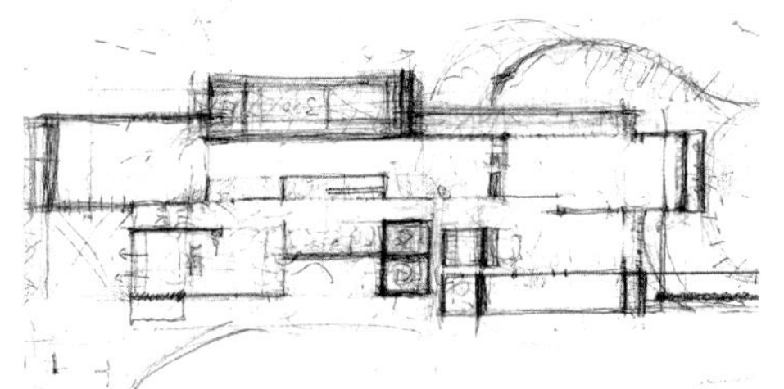

El Prat Royal Golf Club is located on slightly sloping land flanked by linear areas of pinewood and terraced plots. The project for the clubhouse and the adjoining buildings is conceived according to criteria of respect towards and integration within the landscape as a whole, of accessibility, communication and centrality vis-à-vis the golf links *per se*.

The program of the central clubhouse building, based on a detailed study of the topography, is developed on two levels, the service zone being buried, and the technical and installations zone, which is not visible from the outside, being concentrated in the center; using this criterion the entire facade enjoys the view of the landscape.

One accedes to the building from the upper floor at the end of the wooded area intended for parking in, via a large entrance hall from which there runs the building's longitudinal axis of distribution, to the sides of which the more representative functions of the social club are laid out: a games room, a bar with a large terrace with pergola, and entertainment rooms and restaurant, and on the other side spaces intended for offices and administration.

From the entrance hall one accedes by means of an open stairway to a double-height space and to the vestibule of the lower floor, orientated crosswise with regard to the building, in such a way that it opens onto the two orientations facing the landscape. This permits access to the generously proportioned changing-room area of the club members, which functions as a lounge and meeting area. Each one has a built-in lounge, sauna and massage area, and a small covered swimming pool. Sited on this level is the parking area of the electric golf carts and clubs, a small bar and a gym.

The adjoining building, a visitors' changing-room area, the summer bar and a building for kids all back onto a wall that, proceeding from the central building, adapts to the terrain and has a stepped configuration in layout in order to soften its impact on the landscape. It acts as a filter towards the parking area and the open-air swimming pool.

The materials used are white brick and green quartzite, thus accentuating the building's integration in its context, the horizontality of the whole.

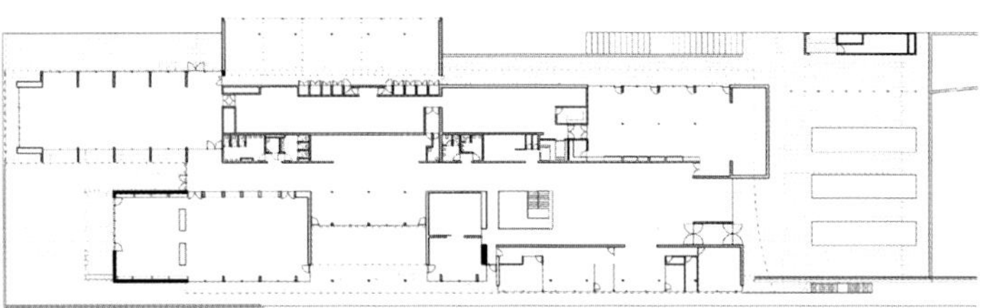

Ground floor plan

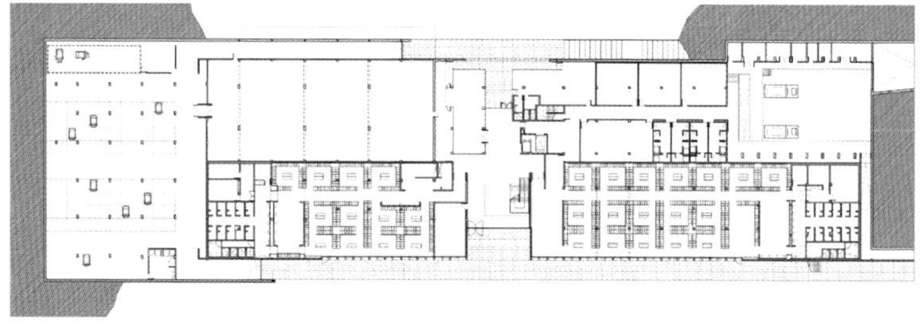

Lockers floor plan

0 1 10

REAL CLUB DE GOLF EL

Golf Course designed by Greg Norman

## Auditorium in Castellón

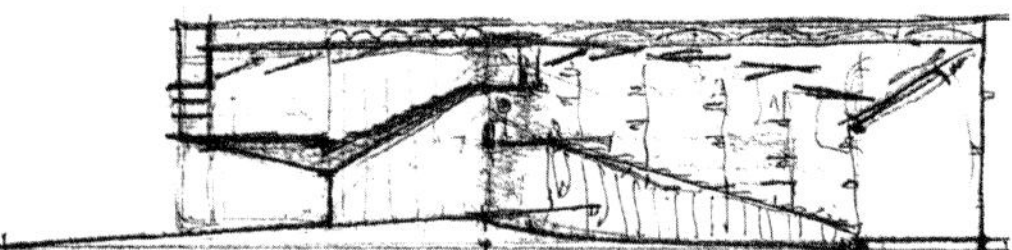

The auditorium project contemplates a permanent dialogue between the exterior space and the building.

The paving of the plaza, gently sloping, invades the auditorium hall through a sequence of spaces that cause a transition between the exterior and the interior below the listening rooms, forming lobbies, foyers, and relationship spaces. The general volume is broken down into four pieces. In the first ones, there are the audition rooms.

The major for symphonic music, the minor for chamber music. Under these rooms are located the hall, the waiting areas and the bar.

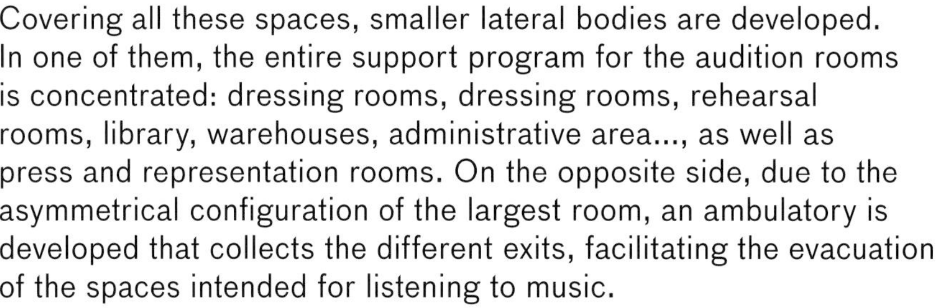

Covering all these spaces, smaller lateral bodies are developed. In one of them, the entire support program for the audition rooms is concentrated: dressing rooms, dressing rooms, rehearsal rooms, library, warehouses, administrative area..., as well as press and representation rooms. On the opposite side, due to the asymmetrical configuration of the largest room, an ambulatory is developed that collects the different exits, facilitating the evacuation of the spaces intended for listening to music.

Next to these pieces or volumes and forming a single set with the auditorium, are the rooms for conferences, social events, exhibition halls and meetings.

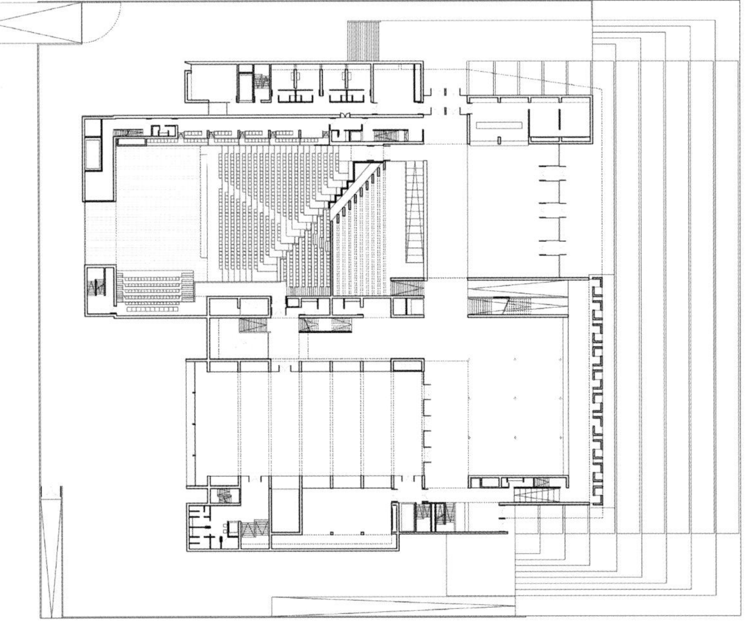

Level 0

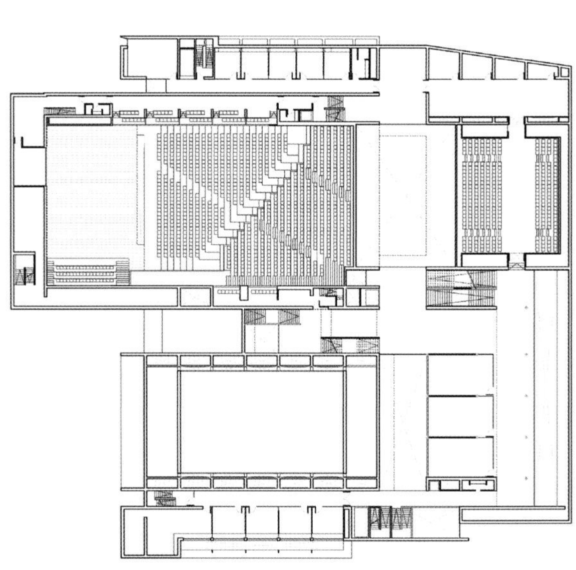

Level 4

0 10

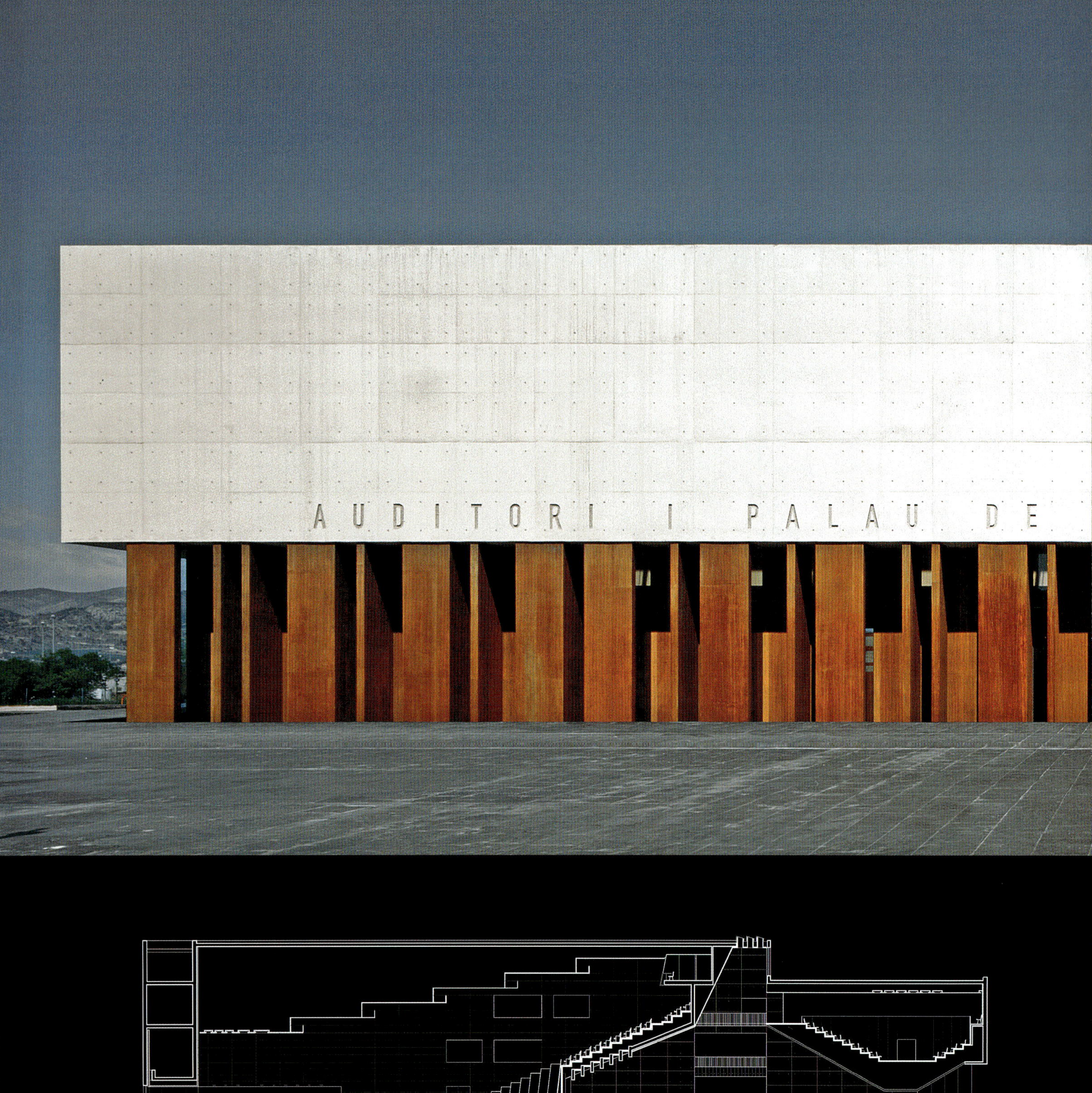


Longitudinal section

NGRESSOS DE CASTELLÓ

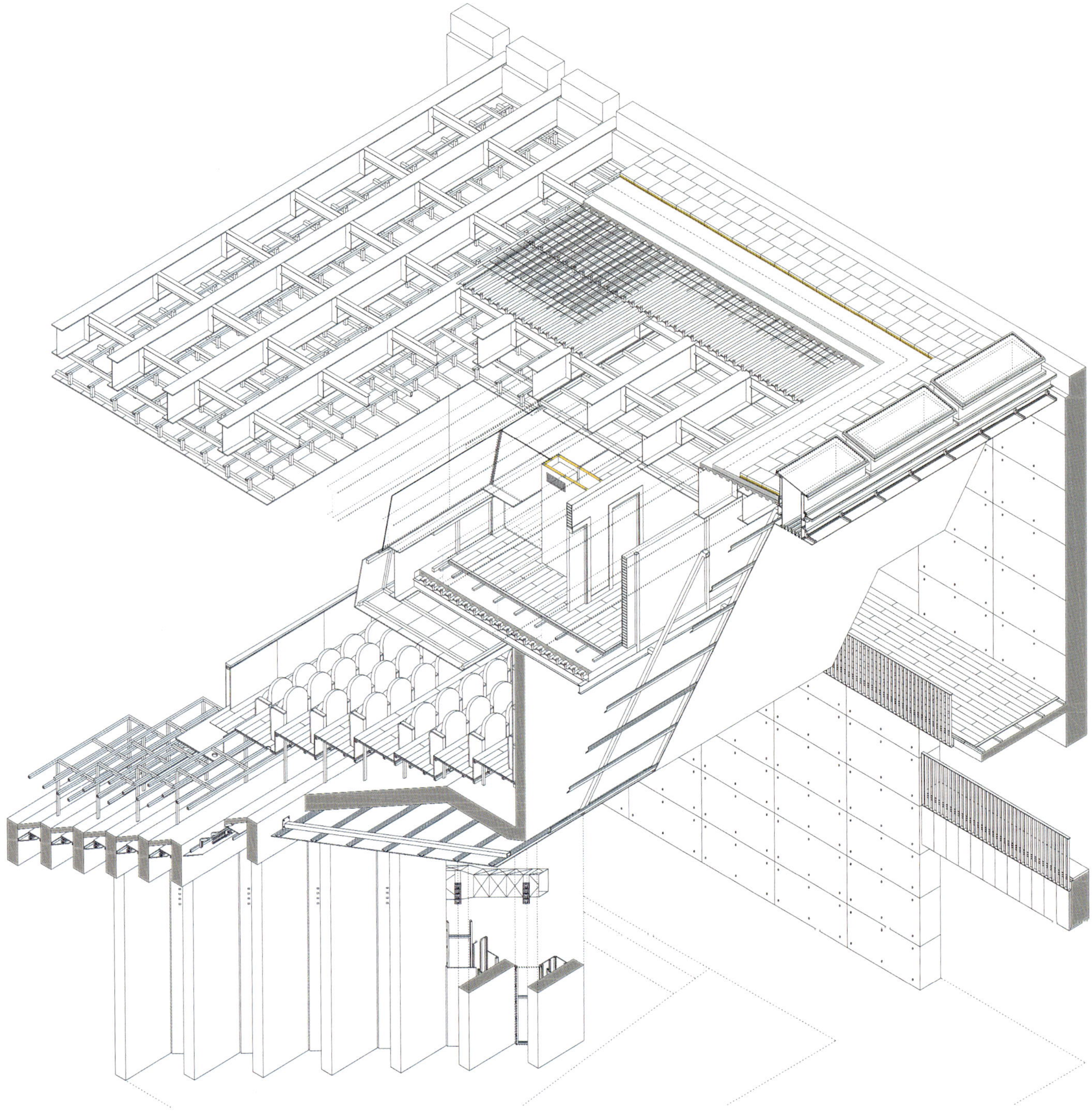

Axonometric constructive section

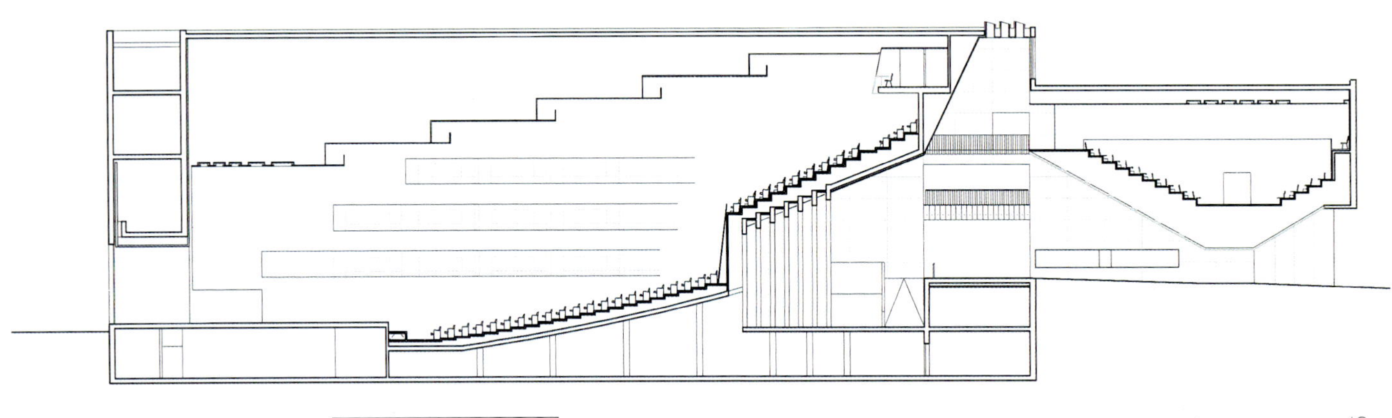


Auditorium section

# Also built

Five Houses 1979
L'Estartit. Girona

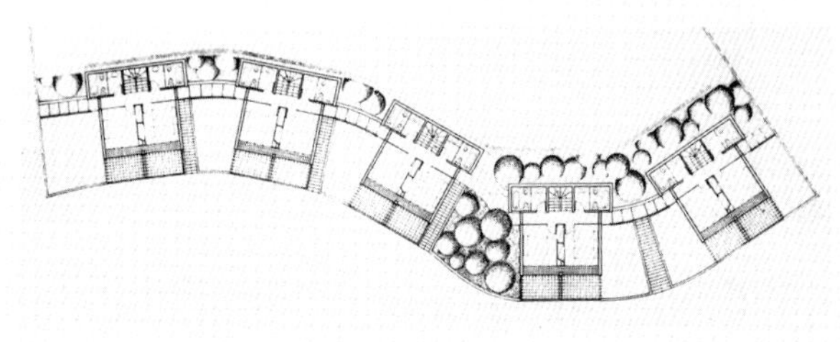

Single Family House 1985
Barcelona

Parking Building 1986
Sitges. Barcelona

Municipal Market 1987
Vilaseca- Salou. Tarragona

CAP Carmel 1988
Barcelona

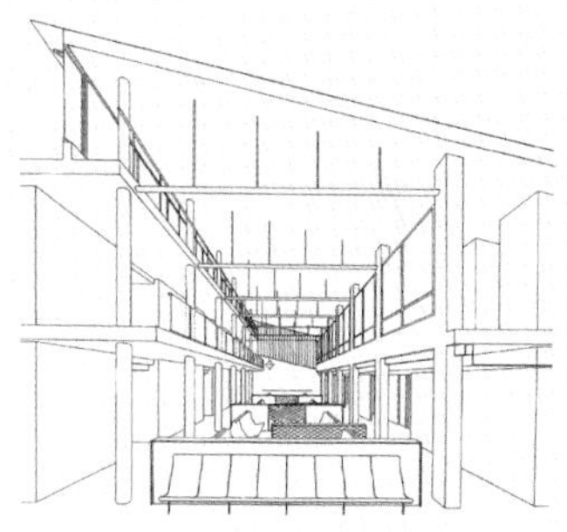

Sports Center 1988
L'Ametlla del Vallès. Barcelona

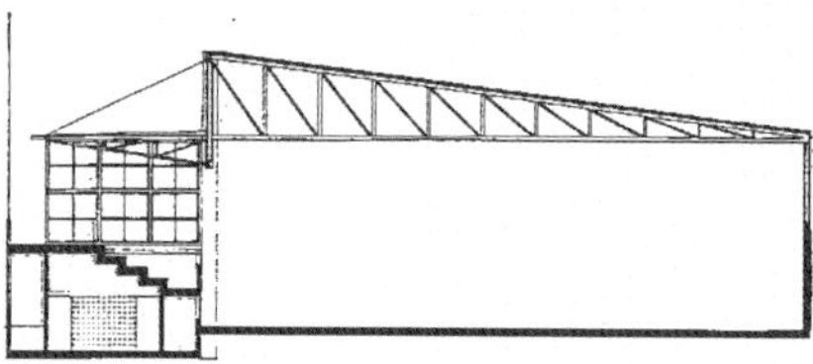

Sports Center 1991
Ciutadella. Menorca

Single Family House 1993
Campelles. Girona

Fisersa Headquarters 1998
Figueres. Girona

Sports Center 1999
Lliçà de Munt. Barcelona

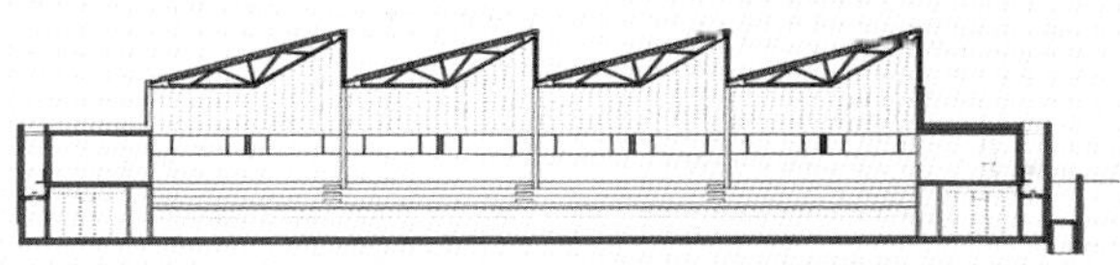

Ter Museum 2000
Manlleu. Barcelona

Four Family Houses 2001
Barcelona

Single Family House 2002
Esplugues de Llobregat. Barcelona

Golf Empordà Hotel 2003
Gualta. Girona

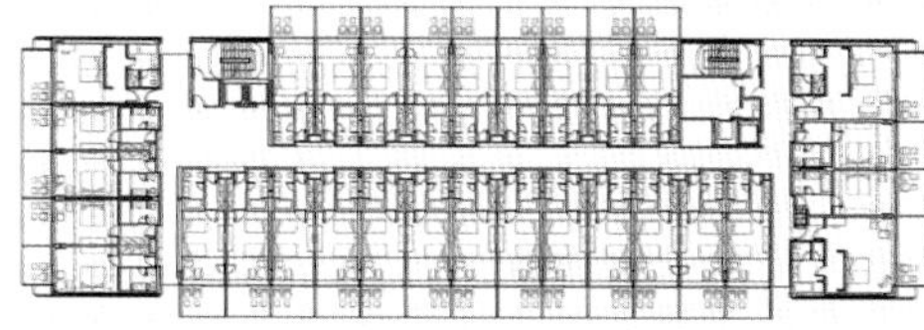

Cuarto Real de Santo Domingo 2004
Granada

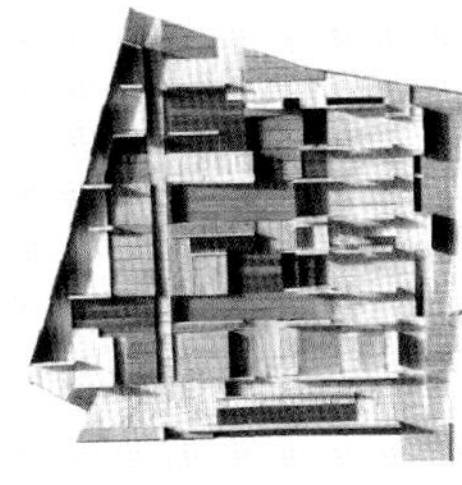

Sant Just Desvern
El Prat del Llobregat

Interactive Maping

# Projects Description

**INSTANT CITY**
LOCATION BARCELONA
ARCHITECTS F. BENDITO – C.FERRATER – J.M.PRADA POOL

**EL PORT BUILDING**
LOCATION L'ESTARTIT (GIRONA)
ARCHITECT CARLOS FERRATER

**GUIX DE LA MEDA**
LOCATION L'ESTARTIT (GIRONA)
ARCHITECT CARLOS FERRATER

**GARBÍ BUILDING**
LOCATION L'ESTARTIT (GIRONA)
ARCHITECT CARLOS FERRATER

**MOLINET HOUSE**
LOCATION L'ESTARTIT (GIRONA)
ARCHITECT CARLOS FERRATER

**YATCH CLUB. L'ESTARTIT**
LOCATION L'ESTARTIT
ARCHITECTS C. FERRATER – G. RODRÍGUEZ – J.DÍAZ

**SANT JUST PARK**
LOCATION SANT JUST DESVERN (BARCELONA)
ARCHITECT CARLOS FERRATER

**SANT JUST. HOUSES IN A FOREST**
LOCATION SANT JUST DESVERN (BARCELONA)
ARCHITECT CARLOS FERRATER

**SPORTS CENTER IN TORROELLA DE MONTGRÍ**
LOCATION TORROELLA DE MONTGRÍ (GIRONA)
ARCHITECTS C. FERRATER – A. PLA – J. MONER

**TORREBLANCA GARDEN**
LOCATION ST. JUST DESVERN – ST. FELIU LLOBREGAT – ST. JOAN DESPÍ (BARCELONA)
ARCHITECTS C. FERRATER – N. CINNAMOND

**CONSELL COMARCAL DEL BAIX LLOBREGAT**
LOCATION SANT JUST DESVERN (BARCELONA)
ARCHITECTS C. FERRATER – X. GÜELL

**PROTOTYPE SCHOOL IN LLORET**
LOCATION LLORET DE MAR (GIRONA)
ARCHITECTS C. FERRATER – J. GUIBERNAU

**BERTRAN 67 – BERTRAN 113**
LOCATION BERTRAN 67 – BERTRAN 113 (BARCELONA)
ARCHITECT CARLOS FERRATER

**LOLA RESTAURANT**
LOCATION BARCELONA
ARCHITECTS CARLOS FERRATER

**GRAPHIC SPACE. SUBIRÀ**
LOCATION GRÀCIA DISTRICT (BARCELONA)
ARCHITECTS Y. CONDE – C. FERRATER – J. ENRICH

**LAWYERS ASSOCIATION OF CATALUNYA**
LOCATION ROGER DE LLÚRIA, 106-108 (BARCELONA)
ARCHITECTS C.FERRATER – E.MATEU – J.GUIBERNAU
I.ARQUER (INTERIOR DESIGN)

**BINISAFUA HOUSE**
LOCATION BINISAFUA (MENORCA)
ARCHITECT CARLOS FERRATER

**TRIGINER HOUSE**
LOCATION VALLVIDRERA (BARCELONA)
ARCHITECTS C. FERRATER WITH J. GUIBERNAU

**ALONSO-PLANAS HOUSE**
LOCATION ESPLUGUES DE LLOBREGAT (BARCELONA)
ARCHITECTS C. FERRATER – J. GUIBERNAU

**TAGOMAGO HOUSE**
LOCATION SANTA EULÀRIA DES RIU (IBIZA)
ARCHITECTS C. FERRATER WITH J. GUIBERNAU

**VALL D'HEBRON OLYMPIC AREA**
LOCATION VALL D'HEBRON (BARCELONA)
ARCHITECTS C. FERRATER – J.M. CARTAÑÁ – R. SUSO

**OLYMPIC HOTEL**
LOCATION DIAGONAL AVENUE (BARCELONA)
ARCHITECTS C. FERRATER – J.M. CARTAÑÁ WITH A. DE SALAS

**BOTANICAL GARDEN OF BARCELONA**
LOCATION MONTJUÏC MOUNTAIN (BARCELONA)
ARCHITECTS C. FERRATER – B. FIGUERAS – J.L. CANOSA

**POBLENOU OLYMPIC AREA**
LOCATION POBLENOU DISTRICT (BARCELONA)
ARCHITECTS CARLOS FERRATER WITH J.M. MONTANER – B. FIGUERAS – J. SAMSÓ

**BANYOLES OLYMPIC AREA**
LOCATION BANYOLES (GIRONA)
ARCHITECTS C. FERRATER WITH A. DA COSTA – J. CAPLAN

**HOUSE-STUDIO IN LLAMPAIES**
LOCATION LLAMPAIES (GIRONA)
ARCHITECTS C. FERRATER WITH J. GUIBERNAU

**IMPIVA TECHNOLOGICAL PARK**
LOCATION CASTELLÓN DE LA PLANA
ARCHITECTS C.FERRATER – C.BENTO – J.SANAHUJA
WITH C.MARTÍN – C. ESCURA

**UAB LIBRARY COMPLEX**
LOCATION BARCELONA
ARCHITECT CARLOS FERRATER

**FITNESS CENTER**
LOCATION DIAGONAL AVENUE (BARCELONA)
ARCHITECT CARLOS FERRATER

**MOVIE STUDIO**
LOCATION SANT JUST DESVERN (BARCELONA)
ARCHITECTS CARLOS FERRATE WITH J. GUIBERNAU

**ENLARGEMENT OF THE CIMITERO DEI SAN MICHELE**
LOCATION VENICE (ITALY)
ARCHITECTS C.FERRATER – E.MANTESE WITH C. EUSSEPI

**MUSÉE DES CONFLUENCES**
LOCATION LYON (FRANCE)
ARCHITECTS C. FERRATER – B. DUMETIER
WITH A. PEÑÍN – N. AYALA – J. RODRÍGUEZ

**ARTABRIA MUSEUM**
LOCATION A CORUÑA
ARCHITECTS C. FERRATER WITH J.TRIAS DE BES

**CAMP NOU STADIUM**
LOCATION BARCELONA
ARCHITECTS OAB. C.FERRATER – B.FERRATER
S.V.C & S.V & A.V – E.SERRA – LL.VIVES – J.CARTAGENA
ARUP SPORT – J. PARRISH – M. SIMPSON

**FRONTAURA WINERY**
LOCATION TORO (ZAMORA)
ARCHITECTS OAB. C. FERRATER-X. MARTÍ

**ATAPUERCA MILESTONE**
LOCATION BURGOS
ARCHITECTS OAB – C.FERRATER – B.FERRATER

**CATALONIA CONVENTION CENTER**
LOCATION DIAGONAL AVENUE (BARCELONA)
ARCHITECTS C. FERRATER – J.M. CARTAÑA – A. PEÑÍN
STRUCTURE J. CALVO – A. CARRASCO
ACOUSTICS H. ARAU

**INTERNATIONAL JC DECAUX HEADQUARTERS**
LOCATION MADRID
ARCHITECTS CARLOS FERRATER
WITH J. GUIBERNAU – C. BOYER

**SOCIAL SERVICES CENTER – PUBLIC SPACE – MULTI HOUSING**
LOCATION ALIBEI–ROGER DE FLOR – NÀPOLS (BARCELONA)
ARCHITECTS OAB – C. FERRATER – L.FERRATER

**EL PRAT ROYAL GOLF CLUB**
LOCATION TERRASSA (BARCELONA)
ARCHITECTS CARLOS FERRATER
WITH J. GUIBERNAU – N. AYALA

**AUDITORIUM IN CASTELLÓN**
LOCATION CASTELLÓN DE LA PLANA
ARCHITECTS C. FERRATER – C. MARTÍN – J. SANAHUJA – C. ESCURA WITH A. GÓMEZ – R. PASCUAL

**FIVE HOUSES IN L'ESTARTIT**
LOCATION L'ESTARTIT (GIRONA)
ARCHITECT CARLOS FERRATER

**SINGLE FAMILILY HOUSE**
LOCATION AVDA. PEARSON (BARCELONA)
ARCHITECT CARLOS FERRATER

**PARKING BUILDING IN SITGES**
LOCATION SITGES (BARCELONA)
ARCHITECTS C. FERRATER – J.L. CANOSA

**MUNICIPAL MARKET IN VILASECA-SALOU**
LOCATION VILASECA – SALOU (TARRAGONA)
ARCHITECTS C. FERRATER – J.L. CANOSA

**CAP CARMEL**
LOCATION EL CARMEL (BARCELONA)
ARCHITECTS CARLOS FERRATER WITH A. DE SALAS

**L'AMETLLA SPORTS CENTER**
LOCATION L'AMETLLA DEL VALLÈS (BARCELONA)
ARCHITECTS C. FERRATER – J.L. CANOSA

**CIUTADELLA SPORTS CENTER**
LOCATION CIUTADELLA (MENORCA)
ARCHITECTS C. FERRATER – A. PETSCHEN – J.PONS

**SINGLE FAMILY HOUSE IN CAMPELLES**
LOCATION CAMPELLES (GIRONA)
ARCHITECTS CARLOS FERRATER WITH J. OLIVELLÁ

**FISERSA HEADQUARTERS**
LOCATION FIGUERES (GIRONA)
ARCHITECT CARLOS FERRATER

**LLIÇÀ SPORTS CENTER**
LOCATION LLIÇÀ D'AMUNT (BARCELONA)
ARCHITECTS C. FERRATER – J. GUIBERNAU

**TER MUSEUM**
LOCATION MANLLEU (BARCELONA)
ARCHITECTS C. FERRATER – J.M. MONTANER

**FOUR FAMILY HOUSES**
LOCATION AVDA. REINA ELISENDA (BARCELONA)
ARCHITECTS C. FERRATER – J. GUIBERNAU

**SINGLE FAMILY HOUSE (NOLLA HOUSE)**
LOCATION ESPLUGUES DE LLOBREGAT (BARCELONA)
ARCHITECTS C. FERRATER – J. GUIBERNAU

**GOLF EMPORDÀ HOTEL**
LOCATION GUALTA (GIRONA)
ARCHITECTS C.FERRATER – MARTÍ SARDÀ ARQ.
I. ARQUER (INTERIOR DESIGN)

**CUARTO REAL DE SANTO DOMINGO**
LOCATION GRANADA
ARCHITECTS Y. BRASA & E. JIMÉNEZ – C. FERRATER

Chandigarh. Photo by José Manuel Ferrater

## Carlos Ferrater Lambarri

Born in Barcelona on November 22, 1944. He studied at the Jesuits in Barcelona.

Architect of the Barcelona School of Architecture in 1971. Doctor of Architecture in 1987 with the thesis Singular Work: Continuous Process.

In 2006 he set up, along with Xavier Martí, Lucía Ferrater and Borja Ferrater, the Office of Architecture in Barcelona (OAB), with Núria Ayala as Projects Director.

Academician-Elect of the Real Academia de Belles Arts de Sant Jordi in 2001. Conferred as Doctor honoris causa by the University of Trieste in 2005. Awarded the 2009 National Architecture Award by the Spanish Ministry of Housing for his overall career. Since december 2011 member of the Royal Institute of British Architects (International RIBA Felowship). Gold Medal of the Fine Arts (Spain, 2019).

President of ADI-FAD (1985-1987). President of IN-FAD (1989-1990). President of ARQ-INFAD (1991-1992). President of the FAD Awards for Architecture and Interior Design in 2001, President of the awards of the IV Biennial of Spanish Architecture, Member of the Scientific Committee of the Ibero-American Architecture Biennial. In the year 2000 he participates in the closing of the VIII Alvar Aalto Symposium with the conference "Architecture in the year zero". He has given lectures and master classes at institutions and universities around the world.

### CV Professional

He has won five FAD Awards and has been a finalist more than thirty times. He also won the 1999 and 2008 City of Barcelona Award, the 2002 City of Madrid Award, the 2005 Brunel International Architecture and Engineering Award, prize awarded by the Danish Royal Family. He has four times been a finalist for the Mies van der Rohe Award and nominated in seven occasions. He has received the 2001 Spanish Architecture Award for the Catalonia Conventions Center and the 2011 Spanish Award for the Benidorm Waterfront, the 2006 Dedalo Minosse International Award in Vicenza, the 2006 Decade Award and the 2007 International Flyer Award. The 2008 RIBA International Award was given to his Editorial MP monograph, among others. He received a mention in the X Biennial of Spanish Architecture and urbanism in 2009 and in the Urban Public Space European Award 2010 for the Benidorm Waterfront which also won the FAD 2010, the Chicago Athenaeum International Architecture Award "best global design" 2010 and the CEMEX 2011. First Prize at the European Garden Awards 2019/20 (European Garden Heritage) in the category of Innovative Contemporary Concept for the JBB.

More than 25 monographs have been published on his work, including the monograph published by the Ministry of Housing after winning the National Architecture Award.

He was a guest exhibitor in the International Pavilion and the Spanish Pavilion at the 2004 Venice Biennale, and was invited by the MoMA, New York, to participate in the exhibition On-Site: New Architecture in Spain, and to exhibit his work in a one-man show at the Illinois Institute of Technology's Crown Hall in Chicago, the Bilbao Fine Arts Museum, the Israel Institute of Technology, the College of Architects of Catalonia, the Foundation of the College of Architects of Madrid and the Acquario Romano.

Beginning in June 2012, many models and original drawings of the Benidorm Waterfront have been chosen to form part of the collection of the Centre National d'Art et de Culture Georges Pompidou, along with the Iberia building on Passeig de Gràcia and the Barcelona Botanical Garden. Some of them have been exhibited in the temporary exhibition of the Pompidou "Modern Utopias" in Malaga. Also several original drawings are part of the Avery Collection of Columbia University.

*"To trace the evolution of Ferrater's work is to sense, simultaneously, the absorption of the outside influences and the emergence of guiding themes. His commitments to tight functional planning and to vocabulary based upon structure place him broadly in a "Rationalist" lineage, although the utilitarian is clearly regarded as a basic discipline in the search for an art of proportion, space, colour and light".*

— William Curtis (1989)

*"In his case, key predecessors have been Coderch in the 1950s (with the organic abstraction and his marvellous splayed walls), Sert in the 1930s (with his researches into modern typologies for the industrial Mediterranean city) and Gaudí at the turn of he century (with his topographical geometries, and his responses to nature)".*

— William Curtis (2000)

### CV Academic

He was appointed professor at the Universitat Politècnica de Catalunya following a competitive process in 2004 (Serra Húnter Chair) and has formed part of the body of university professors since 2009.

Professor of Designs at the Barcelona School of Architecture (ETSAB) of the Universitat Politècnica de Catalunya, he was co-director of the "Càtedra Blanca" professorial chair in Barcelona in the period 1999-2014.

From the Càtedra Blanca, he organised the Barcelona-Madrid (ETSAB) and Madrid-Barcelona (ETSAM) Conferences with the title "Two ways of understanding the city and understanding the culture and teaching of architecture", together with Alberto Peñín. He edited the Càtedra Blanca's publications until the 2005-2006 academic year, including the monograph "Last But One", as well as the Palimpsesto journal, of which 24 issues have now been published, together with a large format compilation of the first 20 issues.

Alongside this, he has been a visiting professor giving seminars, lectures and chairing thesis and competitive examination tribunals at various universities, both in Spain and abroad. His academic activity includes organising the seminar "Critical research, the search for authenticity" with William Curtis (ETSAB); directing the postgraduate programme "Design and experience" (ETSAB); and acting as teacher and director of the summer courses "The small dimension" and "Architecture: enunciating the design" at the Universidad Internacional Menéndez Pelayo in Santander in 1993 and 1995, with Félix Arranz as Academic Secretary.

He has been visiting professor at the most important Spanish Schools of Architecture, as well as L'Ecole Polytechnique Federale in Lausanne; the Universidad Pontificia Bolivariana in Medellín (Colombia); the Universidad de Córdoba (Argentina); the Institut Supèrieur in Sant Luc, Wallonia; the Facultad de Arquitectura in Buenos Aires; the Amsterdam Academy; the Faculty of Architecture and Urban Planning at the Universidade de São Paulo, Brazil; the Instituto Universitario di Architectura di Venezia; the TU in Berlin; the Universidad Javeriana in Bogotá; Washington University; Saint Louis University; the Politecnico de Milano; the Accademia di Architettura di Mendrisio and the AA of London, among others.

*"Carlos Ferrater's academic thoughts embody and renew the tradition of the Barcelona school. Its origin is the profession and its destiny the elaboration of a retroactive intellectual space, skeptical of speculation or erudition, committed to its social, technical and urban environment, but without abandoning its autonomy or relegating personal creativity. The critical attitude of his architecture extends to his most genuine academic contributions; the opening to the technical reality with the first business chair or with the research on the architect-engineer relationship, the innovation of teaching and research publications, or the reinterpretation of the history of the modern movement through complex geometries. Architecture at the centre, with no escape, for students under a threshold of commitment, intuition and knowledge".*

— Alberto Peñín (2022)

Published by
ACTAR Publishers
New York_Barcelona
www.actar.com

Edited by
Núria Ayala

Text supervision & Archive OAB–CF
Judith Gabarró

Translation
Paul Hammond
Simon Berrill

Graphic design and production
Actar Publishers

Graphic documentation
Estudio OAB

Photographs
OAB would like to thank the photographers who have shot our work, especially Lluís Casals, Aleix Bagué and Joan Guillamat

Lluís Casals 35-37, 39-45, 47-55, 65-69, 71-73, 75-77, 86-87, 89, 95-99, 102, 107, 109-115, 118-121, 123-129, 131-135, 142-157, 159-165, 167-179, 186-187, 194-195, 198-203, 217-223, 227, 229-237, 239-247, 251-261

Aleix Bagué 137-141, 205, 208-215, 269, 271, 279-293, 295-305, 307-317, 319-331, 333-341, 343-347

Joan Guillamat 80-81, 90-92, 101, 104-105, 117, 188-191, 193, 197, 224-225

Ferràn Freixa 57-59, 61



U.S ISBN: 978-1-638400-21-9
PCN, Library of Congress Control Number: 2022936077

Printing and bound
in the European Union

Distribution
Actar Distribution
New York_Barcelona
www.actar.com

New York
440 Park Avenue South,
17th Floor
NEW YORK, NY 10016, USA
T +1 2 129 662 207
salesnewyork@actar-d.com

Barcelona
Roca i Batlle 2-4
08023 BARCELONA, Spain
T +34 933 282 183
eurosales@actar-d.com